CW00341898

The Science
of Politics

The Science of Politics

Maurice Saatchi

Weidenfeld & Nicolson

LONDON

First published in Great Britain in 2001
by Weidenfeld & Nicolson

© 2001 Maurice Saatchi
The moral right of Maurice Saatchi to be identified as the
author of this work has been asserted in accordance with
the Copyright, Designs and Patents Act of 1988.

All rights reserved. No part of this publication may be
reproduced, stored in a retrieval system, or transmitted
in any form or by any means, electronic, mechanical,
photocopying, recording, or otherwise, without the prior
permission of both the copyright owner and the above
publisher of this book.

A CIP catalogue record for this book is available
from the British Library.

ISBN 0 297 60768 5

Printed in Great Britain by
Butler & Tanner Ltd, Frome and London

Weidenfeld & Nicolson

The Orion Publishing Group Ltd
Orion House
5 Upper Saint Martin's Lane
London, WC2H 9EA

To
Josephine Hart

Contents

Acknowledgements

I would like to thank Professor Jean Aitchison and Peter Stothard, whose invitation to give the Times Lecture at Worcester College, Oxford, prompted the speculations which led to this book.

I also thank Dr Isolde Victory in the House of Lords Library, to which I was lucky enough to have access. In answer to the simple question, 'What has been written about the Conservative Party and economics?' the Library gave me a reading list that occupied two memorable summers and provided the basis of the histories of the Labour and Conservative parties. I am wholly indebted to the esteemed authors of these works and all the others listed in the bibliography. The House of Lords Library is a remarkable institution both for its scholarship and its efficiency.

To Tessa Keswick, the Director of the Centre for Policy Studies, I owe all that a nervous apprentice could ask: encouragement to put pen to paper. Tessa gave me the honour of commissioning two pamphlets for the CPS – *The War of Independence* and *The Bad Samaritan*. Without the support of the CPS this book would not exist.

I offer a special thank you to Lord Thorneycroft (in memoriam), Lord Parkinson, Lord Tebbit, Chris Patten and Brian Mawhinney for allowing me to sit at their feet through elections thin and thick.

The book would be pointless without the final chapter, which was the result of a happy collaboration with three extraordinary people.

Dr Peter Warburton, latterly Chief Economist at the Robert Fleming Investment Bank, and now a founding Partner of

Economic Perspectives, was the co-author of our two CPS pamphlets. Peter's encyclopaedic knowledge of the highways and byways of the UK's labyrinthine tax system is awesome to behold. The good ideas in this book are his and the rest are mine alone.

I was introduced to Peter via Steve Hilton, who joined Saatchi & Saatchi as an undergraduate and worked with me on the last two election campaigns. I let Steve slip through my fingers when he set up his own business. Steve knows more about politics than people twice his age and I still don't know how I survive without him.

I have been working at the same bench with Jeremy Sinclair – metaphorically, now literally – for longer than I care to remember. He founded Saatchi & Saatchi with my brother and I, and then M&C Saatchi. When occasionally distracted from the latest market share of this or that washing-up liquid we were occupied by five election campaigns and by some of the thoughts now contained in this book. Jeremy is simply the wisest man I know.

All three of them have something in common. Like Supermen, beneath their mild-mannered exteriors beats a passionate heart, bursting for reform.

Alison Provan and David Atkinson, my editor and copyeditor at Weidenfeld & Nicolson, removed dozens of errors of omission and commission.

Carol Jackson typed this manuscript in what was known as her 'spare time', of which there was none. I am most grateful to her.

Preface

When Lord Weidenfeld asked me to describe the prospects for the British Conservative Party in the new century of course I said yes, I would have a go, but I knew at the time that I would approach this particular subject with trepidation. Because when it comes to forecasting the politics of the next week a certain humility is appropriate. And as for the next century … that is obviously beyond my ken.

So if my thesis in this book seems a little, shall we say, simplistic, then that is in the hope that simplification, as Isaiah Berlin said, is 'not always falsification and often serves to crystallize the issues'.

To take my point, readers need only allow me one assumption: that the public is very intelligent, that they can see through a logical flaw in a political argument and that the perpetrator suffers immediate punishment. If readers can accept that, then they might be willing to share with me a view of politics as not driven by personality or events, or by Thatcher versus Callaghan or Kinnock vs Major or Blair vs Hague, but as a rational battle where the winner is the one with the best arguments, not the prettiest face.

Introduction

The British Conservative Party has been the most successful political party of the modern era. It has been in government, either alone or in coalitions dominated by it, for seventy of the 109 years separating Benjamin Disraeli's death and Margaret Thatcher's resignation.

No other European party of the Right operating within a mass electoral system has equalled this achievement, and on the Left only the Swedish Social Democrats have come close. At the end of the twentieth century – what Arthur Seldon called the 'Conservative Century' – the Conservative Party could have been forgiven for considering itself Britain's natural party of government.

The British Conservatives spent the twentieth century with a crystal-clear identity, successfully depicting their socialist opponents as totalitarian wolves in the clothing of constitutional sheep. It was the Conservatives who developed all the winning arguments of our time. They presented a wonderful '–ism': Conservatism. When everyone said that there was nothing that could be done with Britain, they disagreed.

They were proud of Conservative economics and what it could do. For example, they said that 'caring that works costs cash' – the Good Samaritan showed that first you need the money in order to do the good works. They said that 'a bigger cake means a bigger slice for everyone'. But first you had to create the wealth to make the cake bigger. They said that 'a rising tide lifts all ships'. They said that lower tax was good – for moral reasons, because it meant more freedom and choice for individuals; and for economic reasons, because, ironically, lower tax rates meant higher tax revenues and more wealth-creation. As

Mrs Thatcher summed it up at the end of the twentieth century, 'the facts of life do invariably turn out to be Tory'.

But then, of all things, after a century-long battle against socialism the facts of life turned out to be Labour too. Under Prime Minister Blair's direction Labour's 'Berlin Wall' came down. He embraced free-enterprise capitalism. He welcomed low tax. He respected work. He admired wealth-creation. When Mr Blair went on to offer his beguiling synthesis of capitalism and socialism, two hundred years of Conservative certainty came to an abrupt end. By the turn of the twenty-first century the Labour Party had been ahead in every opinion poll every month for eight years. And the Conservative Party was nursing its biggest intellectual headache in 200 years.

So can this be another 'Conservative Century'?

Some people say that will be decided by events. They observe governments blown off course daily by the slings and arrows of outrageous political fortune. They conclude that planning the future in politics is for the birds, because the best-laid plans will be overtaken by unforeseen events. A scientist, however, might say that this view overlooks the possibility that the events themselves may be determined by greater forces which can be understood and, if understood, controlled – that laws govern the fall of parties from power as they do the fall of apples from trees.

Those who fall in politics often turn to psychoanalysis for an explanation and treatment. 'It is actually possible to bring about the disappearance of the painful symptoms of the illness,' Freud said, 'if the patient can be brought to remember on what occasions, and in what connection, the symptoms first appeared.' Devotees of Freud, seeking the origin of the Conservative Party's fall, usually find a folk-memory of collective guilt. Matricide is a messy business, demanding retribution. So the instinct for self-destruction will continue until the body has sufficiently punished itself for the 'murder' of Margaret Thatcher.

But Freud himself would have gone further. He thought it was possible to discover the strict mental determinants of every smallest detail of the processes of the human mind – of even minor and apparently arbitrary physical acts such as forgetting, errors in spite of better knowledge, slips of the tongue, slips of the pen, falls, misreadings, mishaps, and all manner of misfortunes. For Freud, someone who is accident-prone is so for deeper reasons, usually related to occurrences far back in childhood. Churchill agreed: 'The further backward you look, the further forward you can see.'

Therefore, undeterred by the Russian proverb 'If you live in the past, you'll lose an eye', and buoyed up by Solzhenitsyn's amendment of it to read 'If you ignore the past, you'll lose both eyes', I embarked on a voyage of discovery (for me) through Conservative history from infancy to the present day to find the thinking that illuminated Conservative success, and the eternal truth of Conservative identity.

Armed with self-knowledge, Churchill said it is possible for a leader to 'make the weather'. Bismarck said that statesmanship means 'to hear the rustle of God's mantle passing through history and catch his coat-tail for a few steps'. But if your name is not Churchill or Bismarck, how do you hear it? Is there a special hearing-aid? Is that rustling sound His coat or just the fall of autumn leaves? And if you do hear it, how can you catch it and keep hold of it?

To address these questions, this book begins in Chapter One by asking whether there is, or can be, a science of politics. The next two chapters consider the origin and nature of Labour and Conservative answers to that question. They show how their different responses have been determined by their different genetic inheritance, how the very terms Left and Right can be defined by their answers: on the Left, romanticism; on the Right, cynicism.

To the romantic mind of the Left there is much that is objectionable about the state of the world. It thinks that, by an act of will, people can make things better. Labour's romanticism leads to activism. It has a linear approach. It sees itself at a point A – misery – and wants to get to point B – happiness. It makes a plan to get there. Chapter Two shows how such thinking led to the birth of the Labour Party and asserts that however much Labour moves from 'Old' to 'New' it cannot shake off its childhood influences – the romantic belief in human ability to change the political environment by scientific planning.

To the cynical mind of the Right, in contrast, it is not necessary for politics to be a science because it is not planning on going anywhere in particular. Nor is it desirable, because it might raise in the public false expectations of what can be achieved by 'the art of the possible'. With a shrug of the shoulders often mistaken for heartlessness, Conservatives deny that any plan or act of will on the part of mere humans can build a new Jerusalem.

In Chapter Three we find that Conservatives reject the scientific view of history – that politics is made by the 'man with a mission', or that 'one man with an idea is worth a thousand armies'. Conservative cynicism leads to pragmatism. Conservatives can settle for the way things are because they see *grands projets* as *folies de grandeur*, based on a mistaken assumption about the powers and functions of modern man.

Such is the basis of the Great Divide in British politics: how the Left came to be seen as 'caring but incompetent', and the Right as 'efficient but cruel'. The book argues that between the failed romanticism of the Left – the disillusionment of lost dreams – and the cynicism of the Right – the sigh of acceptance at the wicked ways of the world – the public is left high and dry, sceptical of all politics and politicians.

The final chapter then attempts something like Baron Munchausen's feat in extricating himself from a swamp by pulling on his whiskers: it proposes a synthesis to appeal to utopian theories as well as practical necessities. It predicts, as a stark fact of twenty-first century life, that government and citizen will have something in common: they will both be short of money.

The government does not have enough of it for the best health service, schools, roads and suchlike; and the citizen does not have enough for a good pension, medical care in old age, university fees and so on. So they torture each other. Governments put up tax, which reduces individual incomes and creates more dependence on the state. And citizens claim more state benefits to compensate. And so it goes on until the government is claiming billions of pounds a year in taxes from citizens who also claim billions of pounds a year in benefits from the government.

Instead, the book offers a romantic dream to which even the cynic might aspire, in which twenty-first century technology heralds a New Enlightenment that will bring greater independence for all. After a grown-up conversation, government and citizen agree to go their separate ways, each delighted to be rid of the other.

.

1

Is there a science of politics?

'If science can predict eclipses,' Professor Popper asked, 'why can't it predict revolutions?'

In so-called political science there has always been a deep longing for general rules about the real world as robust as the laws of physics. There has been a stream of heroic attempts to turn the study of politics into a natural science – to find the laws.

The first person who tried to discover such general laws of politics was Plato. But sadly, in Plato's allegory of the human condition we were tied to chains in a dark cave, able to see a passing parade of objects we *thought* were real but which were in fact only the shadows cast by the objects.

Is what we perceive real?

All of us know that the sensations produced by the same object can vary with the circumstances. Lukewarm water will seem hot to a cold hand, and cold to a hot hand. Colours look very different through a microscope. Even the sun in the heavens we see only as it was eight minutes before.

For early theologians, this state of ignorance was a fitting punishment because in humanity's fallen state after Eden we were denied full knowledge, which was to be reserved only for God. After all, we only got one bite of the apple, not the whole tree. We would know truth only in the life beyond the grave.

However, there came a time when it was believed that rational methods – observation, experiment, verification – could establish the truth that previously only God possessed. The third dream of René Descartes on 10 November 1619, in the small Bavarian village of Ulm, foresaw a universal method by which all human problems, whether of science, law, or politics, could be solved: the method of reason. The dream pointed to the illumination of the whole of knowledge by systematic, logical computation.

We began to believe in the idea of a science of humanity, which would release us from the darkness of Plato's cave. Ethics, politics, economics, psychology, philosophy would overcome prejudice and superstition and bring us to a utopia of wisdom and happiness where 'men shall beat their swords into ploughshares ... the wolf shall dwell with the lamb, the leopard shall lie down with the kid ... the desert shall rejoice, and blossom as the rose' – an earthly paradise of universal enlightenment.

Unfortunately, it has not worked out quite like that. Instead, we find the inconvenient and stubborn fact that outside Newton's universe, where physical laws govern reality, the world is conditioned by perception. And perception is conditioned by the distorting factors of society, genetics, class, upbringing, and the conscious or unconscious interests of the perceiver. Marx and Freud certainly believed in the power of appearance and illusion over objective reality, that our perception of events is unavoidably determined by forces over which we have no control – Freud's unconscious drives formed in childhood, Marx's class-bound morality.

Philosophers have always sought a path to a version of reality that could be accepted as a universal law or truth. They have wanted to help humankind avoid the chaos of Hobbes' *bellum omnium contra omnes*, the war of all against all. In the doctrine of the church, truth was to be found in the ancient gospels and biblical texts, interpreted for us by a benevolent priesthood. Others were certain that 'good' meant being conducive to human happiness, or moving towards the greatest general good, the *summum bonum*, or achieving the greatest balance of pleasure over pain.

But all these certainties ceased when Professor Ayer pronounced the death of the syllogism as the paradigm of deductive reasoning. He showed that the apparently logical progression 'Pruning roses is good; I prune roses; I am good' fails, because the premise that pruning roses is good is open to question by those who prefer leggy, straggly roses with few blooms. So human perceptions of good and evil, right and wrong, turned out to be just an expression of taste with no objective basis whatsoever – no different from preferring a bombe glacé to a bacon sandwich.

Shakespeare knew as much years ago, when Hamlet said 'There is nothing either good or bad / But thinking makes it so.' Even the perception of physical objects cannot be relied upon: Descartes famously said that he couldn't be sure that the table at which he was sitting was really there, because the only thing about which he could be certain was that while he was thinking that the table might *not* be there after all, it was definite that *he* was there looking at it, because he thought he was.

One of Tom Stoppard's characters explained that although it *appeared* to a casual observer standing on the platform at Paddington station that the train had left Paddington, in fact, 'all the observable phenomena indicated that Paddington had left the train.' It seems that once we describe what we perceive in terms of what we feel or believe – once we express opinions or beliefs, or attempt to offer explanations or descriptions or forecasts – then error, doubt and uncertainty come to the fore.

So it is in those psychological tests that confront subjects with a picture and ask them to describe what they see. In one such test respondents are shown a picture of a crowded underground train in which one man stands brandishing a knife. Different respondents produce quite different explanations of what is happening in the picture. Some say the knifeman is a thief. Others that he is a plain-clothes policeman. Sometimes the man, who is white, is said to be black.

But if white is black, what is real?

In his film *Rashōmon*, Kurosawa showed us four very different versions of 'reality'. In twelfth-century Kyoto, a couple are ambushed: the wife is raped, the husband killed. After the event four people recall the attack. By altering the perspective and order of events for each character, we perceive the *un*reality of their contrasting perceptions. This is perhaps why English law would not rely on *any* of the versions provided by Kurosawa's witnesses. Our legal system prefers the principle of *mens rea*, the guilty mind. What matters is not what was perceived in the eyes of observers, but what was perceived in the mind of the accused.

This failure to pin down reality independent of perception is not due to want of effort. Psychology, sociology, economics, politics have all wanted to attach the designation 'science' to their endeavours, to be the social sciences. The point may be noted at the LSE, where the sign above the front door reads 'the London School of Economics and Political *Science*'.

Social scientists from the LSE and other such institutions have tried to show that they too can verify statements, propositions and putative facts by the results of empirical studies. Buoyed up by Popper's warning that even in the natural sciences predicted correlations do not entail final proof or explanation (the closest approach to proof being a succession of unsuccessful attempts at falsification), scholars in the humanities have long sought a set of general, testable, explanatory propositions applicable to the whole area of collective human behaviour.

For example, the painter Delacroix once proposed as a universal law that if an artist cannot capture in a sketch a man falling from a fifth-floor window before he hits the ground, then that artist would never be capable of monumental work. But the quantitative fetishists among us would argue that to verify this proposition it would be necessary to throw one hundred people out of a window (or is it one person a hundred times?) and observe the results. Think of the fun of deciding who those hundred people might be.

Similarly, the proponents of an objective study of personality have insisted that Freud, like Delacroix, based his generalizations on so few cases that a scientist would blush for him. Instead, a true science of personality would base its theories on actual behavioural measurements. Thus, if the theory was that, say, babies who are breast-fed turn out to be more optimistic in temperament as adults than those who are not, then an experimenter could apply a measurement of optimism to hundreds of people in each group and arrive at a form of verifiable proof.

The father of this quantitative approach to psychology was Professor B. F. Skinner from Harvard. He took the view that all this Freudian nonsense about childhood was so much unscientific mumbo-jumbo. In his more measurable approach people merely responded to certain stimuli: reward and punishment, pleasure and pain. Laboratory rats, he told his students, moved *towards* pleasure, in the form of cheese, and *away* from pain, in the form of an electric shock. These laboratory experiments proved his theory, so he said.

One day at Harvard, Professor Skinner's students found a way to test his theory on him. Skinner's habit during his lectures was to pace from one side of the stage to the other. When he went to the right side his students leaned forward, looked animated and took notes furiously. When he went to the left side, they slumped back in their chairs, looking bored or asleep. Sure enough, towards the end of his lecture, Professor Skinner had conformed to his own reward and punishment theory. His pacing ended and he completed the lecture standing firmly on the right-hand side of the stage.

So if, as scientists tell us, Einstein's paper on the special theory of relativity was originally called 'On the Electrodynamics of Moving Bodies', then this type of work in psychology could be labelled 'On the Psychodynamics of Moving Cheese'. What Professor Skinner overlooked is the ghastly possibility that some human beings are so complicated that they can actually get their cheese from electric shocks.

Economists have, of course, told us that there are measurable and predictable relationships between economic phenomena: that the gradient of certain curves can predict the elasticity of demand for a certain product at a certain price; that a society's marginal propensity to consume will change mathematically in accordance with changes in personal taxation. But if all this were true it would mean that we could banish recession in the same way that we banish whooping-cough. It would mean that the current sight in Britain of simultaneously low inflation and low unemployment must be an optical illusion, because the curves say it can't be done.

In so-called political science, too, you find the same desire for quantification, verification, laws. Machiavelli asserted that politics was a self-contained world with its own system of causes and effects, ascertainable from observation and analysis. But even Machiavelli had to admit that however strict a man was in adherence to his laws at least half of the outcome was due to 'Fortuna', otherwise known as sheer luck.

The materialist determinism first propounded by Marx, in which economics determines politics, found its highest expression in, of all places, Conservative Central Office, where there has always existed a deep longing to turn the study of politics into a natural science – to find the law. The last such effort before the 1997 election stated that movements in real personal disposable income over the *last* twelve months would be followed by movements in householders' net expectations about their financial position in the *next* twelve months, which would be followed by movements in voting intention in favour of the Conservative Party.

This fine theory met the laboratory equivalent of Waterloo at precisely midnight on 1 May 1997. Or let us just say with Professor Popper that the evidence failed to confirm the hypothesis.

Even medical experts have been obliged to recognize the infinite power of human perception to control 'reality'. They say that the act of suicide proves that, in extremis, the human mind is omnipotent. It has ultimate power, even to the point of bringing about the final destruction of the human body. A mere cold or backache – or the perception of them – would pose little problem to such an all-powerful force.

This is presumably why fifty per cent of all the drugs prescribed in the world today are said to be prescribed for conditions that are psychosomatic in origin – in other words, where the physical reality of the symptoms is brought about by afflictions of the mind.

Doctors say that Prozac, for example, is a drug that alters human beings' perception of themselves. Its effect is to overcome feelings of inadequacy or low self-esteem so that the user says, 'I am huge.' It can apparently transform marriages, careers, relationships. But there is a catch. When patients stop the course of tablets they can become confused between their perception of themselves and their own reality. One doctor took a 2 a.m. call from a patient who had recently finished her course of Prozac. Her anguished cry for help was 'Doctor, I am not myself!' But which was the real 'self'? Or is it just that, as the *Rubáiyát* says, 'Myself am heaven and am hell'?

In the end, all attempts to place ethics, politics, economics, art, psychology or any of the humanities within the canons of scientific objectivity have failed. There remains an irremediable tentativeness about the logically perplexing question of what is real.

Perhaps in the end the answer will have to come not from

philosophers but from engineers. It is said that a consortium of Japanese electronics companies has noted with interest the $300 billion spent annually on pharmaceutical products. The companies carried out pilot research in Japan which identified to their satisfaction the electronic movements in the brain associated with human emotions: optimism; pessimism; hope; fear; confidence; anxiety – the very stuff of politics. Each of these perceptions, they found, was linked to a magnetic impulse in the brain – the motherlode. If they could identify them, measure them, then they could change them. They are now looking for the best university research department in the world on which to bestow a grant to continue their research and find, once and for all, a scientific solution to the problem of human happiness.

In the meantime, what can we weak creatures do but accept the uncomfortable fact that much of what seems real to us is governed by our own perceptions? After 2000 years of human progress it seems that the real nature of things remains as inaccessible as it was to Aristotle: 'Fire burns both here and in Persia,' he wrote, 'but what is *thought* just changes before our very eyes.' The decision, he said, 'rests with perception'.

The closest science seems to come to politics is the chaos theory of mathematics, the most potent symbol of which is the butterfly that flaps its wings over the Amazon rainforest ... and sets off an electrical storm over Chicago. But the next time it flaps its wings ... nothing happens.

Political science has not yet found its Newton.

2

Romantics say Yes

But in Britain at the end of the twentieth century that conclusion would not do for five men in a hurry. They were 'hommes à programme' and they were going to put Descartes' romantic dream into practice.

Their motivation was to avoid the agony of another election defeat: 1979; 1983; then after the 1987 election they had gone home 'numb and defeated'. After 1992 they had 'sat miserably alone', full of 'remorse ... guilt'. 'Election defeat', one of them explained, is 'like bereavement; a long empty ache'.

So Messrs Blair, Brown, Mandelson, Campbell and their researcher Philip Gould made a mathematical calculation: to eliminate the negatives associated with their party, neutralize the positives associated with their opponent, and thus end a run of four election defeats in a row. With a cold clear eye, they analysed the weaknesses in their position, 'the damning reasons given for not voting Labour'. They removed them one by one. And declared themselves a 'new' party. 'New', for them, was a one-word strategy. 'New' meant 'not old'. 'Old' was bad, dangerous. So 'new' must be good, safe.

That was it.

No wonder Mr Blair 'grabbed the idea with both hands'. As Mr Gould says, 'the fact that Labour had become New Labour gave people the confidence to make the change'.

And it worked. By the time of the last election of the twentieth century, polls showed that seventy-two per cent of the British public agreed that 'New Labour really deserves to be called new', and that 'A man should not be condemned for a sincere conversion'. Labour's rationalist triumph was complete.

How did they do it?

In Sophocles' play *Oedipus Rex*, Oedipus arrives at Thebes when the city is ravaged by the Sphinx, which has settled on a cliff overlooking the city posing riddles to all who attempt to pass and destroying anyone who gives an incorrect answer.

For the Conservative Party, New Labour was an intellectual Sphinx. It posed a series of four riddles, threatening destruction to those who failed to provide the right answers.

Riddle no. 1: Caring vs Economics

It was the fourth Labour election defeat in a row, in 1992, after a Tory campaign totally focused on economics and tax, that made Labour finally give up socialism, reform themselves into New Labour, and copy the cut of Conservative economic cloth.

Until then, the Conservative critique of Labour had been based on Labour's alleged inability to provide a strong economy. This was a long-standing theme of successful Conservative election campaigns. There was a straight line from 'Post Office Savings in Danger', the Conservative slogan in the 1932 election, through 'Life's better. Don't Let Labour Ruin It' in 1959, 'Labour Isn't Working' in 1979, to 'Labour's Tax Bombshell' in 1992.

There had been a consistent economic focus in Conservative campaigns: that while Labour spokesmen wore their hearts on their sleeve and wanted the parade to slow down to the speed of the slowest participant, the Conservatives preferred a more hard-headed, practical approach to economic matters, best summed up by Iain Macleod: 'The Liberals may dream their dreams. And Labour may scheme their schemes. But we have work to do.' A literal translation was that Conservatives knew how to look after your money and Labour didn't.

But by 1997 New Labour had persuaded the British public

that New Labour really was new, that income tax rates would not be increased and that the economy was safe in their hands. From that day, the mechanism that won four elections in a row broke down. The wires were pulled out.

Most successful political parties have built their success on their economic management credentials. There has long been a direct correlation between voting intention and party ratings on tax and managing the economy.

With the Conservatives' four consecutive election victories a concept had become established in voters' minds. The Conservatives were 'efficient but cruel'. This meant that although Conservatives wore bankers' top-hats and tails, they knew how to look after your money. Labour was 'caring but incompetent'. This meant that although Labour were full of anguish, they did not know how to look after your money. But by May 1997 the double drama of Exchange Rate Mechanism (ERM) exit and Blair entrance had turned this happy mechanism into a devastating intellectual vice for the Conservative Party.

Voters displayed textbook reasoning: 'The Conservatives have run the economy badly (ERM exit, tax rises). And even if they could convince me they have run the economy well (low unemployment, low inflation, etc.), Labour will not ruin it (new, reformed).' So, by 1997, the Conservatives were seen as '*ine*fficient and cruel'. And Labour were 'caring *and* competent'.

The sudden withdrawal of the Conservatives' economic advantage over Labour brought the Conservative Party to a strategic crossroads which tested it to the limit. Because of this convergence of party attitudes to money – the same economic clothes – some Tories began to wonder whether economics, the former Conservative ace of trumps, had lost its potency as a political issue.

All losers face a reappraisal of their strengths and weaknesses. They have a choice between rebuilding their strengths or correcting their weaknesses. In the Conservative case, this meant the party could focus either on rebuilding its traditional strengths – tax and spending – or on correcting its traditional weaknesses – care and compassion.

Soon after the 1997 election some people said that since Labour had neutralized the Conservative Party's advantage on economics, it should neutralize theirs on the 'caring' issues – tit for tat.

First, they argued that economics was no longer a discriminating factor between the parties because Labour had become a 'prudent', 'sound' party too. Second, they said that in any case economics was no longer the prime issue at the start of the twenty-first century because the world had changed. They noted the surveys that showed the proportion of British people willing to pay more tax for better public services had doubled in a decade, from thirty to sixty per cent. They concluded that man cannot live by economics alone.

They said the 1997 election result proved their case. All the economic indicators were positive; interest rates, inflation and unemployment were at record lows; and yet the government lost – according to one historian, 'contradicting all previous theories about the relationship between the economy and government popularity ... a major watershed in modern British politics'. They said the 1997 election sounded the historic death-knell of the materialist determinism first propounded by Marx and long embraced by Conservative Central Office.

Some economists agreed. They said that while there may have been a wealth-creating effect in reducing tax from eighty-three to forty per cent, cutting the top rate of income tax from forty to twenty per cent would not have the same effect. The twenty per cent standard rate, they said, was optimal. So tax-cutting should be taken off the Conservative agenda.

As the new century opened, solid research seemed to favour this postmaterialist approach. Polls showed that the main reason people did not vote Conservative in the 1997 election was that the party was 'out of touch with ordinary people'. Other surveys supported this view.

The only trouble with this analysis was that when the Conservative Party was *winning* elections the number-one 'reason for not voting Conservative' had been 'They are out of touch with people like me'. So the Conservative Party's rating on the dimension of 'caring' did not appear to be the determining factor between electoral success and failure.

During the Conservatives' four successful elections from 1979 to 1992, when voters were asked to choose the 'most important issues facing the country' they invariably chose the 'caring' issues: health, education, and unemployment. On each of those issues, at each of the elections, Labour had a fifteen to thirty point net rating advantage over the Conservative Party. So the top three issues were 'caring' issues. And Labour had a huge advantage on all of them. Yet the Conservative Party still won four elections in a row.

Was that because the public was dim? On the contrary, it was because the public was rational and acted in its own interest. In all exit polls prior to 1997 the number-one 'reason for not voting Labour' was 'My taxes would go up and I would not have very much to show for it'. Therefore, it was logical not to vote Labour.

However, by 1997 Labour leaders had systematically removed that reason for rejecting them. Acting rationally, they had deprived the Conservative Party of its most precious asset, so that by 2000 Labour was ahead on all the major issues – both the economic ones and the 'caring' ones – and the Conservative Party was in intensive care.

What seems to matter most in elections is *perception* – real-life economic issues *as people actually perceive them.*

If we revisit the 1997 election with that model in mind, we find ample proof of the relationship between perceived economic performance and actual electoral results. The record seems to show that only one thing had changed between the 1997 election defeat and the four election victories that had preceded it. There was a forty point turn-around against the Conservatives, from +20 to −20, in answer to the standard Gallup question 'With Britain in economic difficulties which party has the best policies for managing the economy?' The only thing that changed between victory and defeat was the perception of the parties' relative economic competence. On all the other dimensions, the ratings of the parties stayed the same.

It was the economic perceptions that New Labour changed. And that made all the difference.

Riddle no. 2: Right vs Centre

In Deep Blue vs Kasparov in Philadelphia in 1996, the world's strongest chess player faced the world's most powerful chess computer in a challenge match. Deep Blue's programmers were recruited from IBM for a mission with the stated aim of defeating the world champion. With Deep Blue reviewing a hundred million chess positions every second, Kasparov was beaten in the opening game.

One of the things for which Deep Blue had been programmed was to move towards the centre of gravity. It had learned that in the geometry of the chessboard, control of the centre – the four central squares and the eight squares around them – takes precedence; that control of the centre is needed to maintain communication between the two wings, enabling a player to bring unrivalled power to bear over the whole board. Wilhelm Steinitz, the first official world chess champion, on whose scientific principles chess is now based, said it was always good in principle to take an opponent's centre pawn.

With the endgame of the twentieth century approaching, Labour's chess grandmasters wanted their king near the centre. Hence their move, by which Labour, having got itself inside the door of Number Ten, planned to slam it in Conservative faces for ever.

How? By showing that Conservatives were as brain-dead as old-style socialists. This was Labour's 'Third Way', the American way.

The Third Way was 'Beyond Left and Right'. We all knew that old-style socialism was dead because it led to economic chaos. So, we were told, would old-style capitalism. Because it leads to cruel' global markets whose brute force is beyond the control of governments or countries. At a stroke, Conservatives were to be consigned to the same intellectual dustbin of history as communism and Marxism.

Some Tory critics said the Third Way was an empty phrase. But they were the same Tories who dismissed New Labour as an empty phrase. Others said the Third Way was just an intellectual edifice to justify one more theft of Conservative clothes – this time of the fine old Tory virtue of pragmatism. But they were the Tories who actually helped New Labour by telling everyone it was a copy of Conservatism. Others said it was just a splitting of the difference between measures for a strong economy and measures for social justice: a lowering of the temperature; a compromise.

In fact, one of Baroness Thatcher's greatest attributes was her ability to spot an intellectual with an idea and at once see its political potential. That is what Labour was doing with Professor Giddens' idea of the Third Way.

In the old days, the Left said the Right was uncaring about the community. And the Right said the Left was irresponsible about personal freedom and dignity. But at a conference at the New York University Law School at the end of the twentieth century, President Clinton and Prime Minister Blair advised Centre-Left parties on how to win elections. Mr Blair said, 'Politics is about ideas and winning elections. The more coherent the ideas the more the chance of winning.' They said that 'the polarities of Left and Right of the twentieth century would prove an aberration'. They favoured 'activist Government but highly disciplined'.

So they spoke of prudent finance, fiscal responsibility, lower deficits. They spoke of competition, choice and flexibility in public services so that investment in them will pay off, of competition in the education system – testing, grades, ratings. They spoke of tax incentives to study because 'what you earn depends on what you learn', of modernizing social policies like the earned income tax credit in exchange for welfare reform. We heard of plans for tax breaks for long-term value creation, tax breaks for good corporate behaviour, policies for private sector growth.

They said that the market economy was fundamental, but rejected Right-wing neo-liberals who said government should shrink, get out of the way and then all would be well. That assumed, they said, that markets are always more intelligent than governments. But that view pre-dated globalization, which was shaking up all our institutions and had produced an entirely new form of capitalism, beyond the reach of national governments. They spoke of this as the driving platform for the twenty-first century, the agenda that would dominate the first thirty years of the century.

Some Tories dismissed all this as the usual hopes and dreams. But dreams are important. People give credit to someone who has his heart in the right place. In politics, as in law, motive is all. Labour was determined to modernize its appeal to the heart, away from the old idea of equality at any price and the class struggle, to a more realistic and acceptable version.

So maybe Labour's Third Way was just stealing Conservative clothes again. But they intended to polish it up until it shined and to relaunch 'the middle of the road' and 'the art of the possible' as something contemporary, exciting, idealistic, something that combined compassion with ambition, competition with fairness, globalization with community, individual freedom with social justice – every schoolboy's dream, and every voter's dream, too.

Riddle no. 3: Modern vs Traditional

Mr Blair is a devotee of the American political maxim 'you campaign in poetry but you govern in prose'. Scholars define poetry as 'the only possible words in the only possible order'. So New Labour looked for the right word to describe their policy. And there it was, on page seventy-two of the Thesaurus:

> *modernization*: meaning ... 'Contemporary, up-to-date, topical, the latest thing, the in-thing, the new look'.

This was logical, because reason tells you a 'new' party would have 'modern' policies.

And where did that leave the Conservative Party? Conveniently, it was on the same page of the Thesaurus:

> *traditional*: meaning ... 'ancien régime; relic of the past; listed building, ancient monument; museum-piece, antique, heirloom, bygone, Victorian; dodo, dinosaur, old fogey, old fossil, fuddy-duddy, square, old-timer, back-number, has-been'.

Labour calculated that the Conservative Party would be discomfited by not wanting to appear old-fashioned on the one hand, but not wanting to abandon its heritage on the other – that it would be left perched perilously somewhere along the continuum between 'modern' and 'traditional'.

The deification of the modern was the theme of the last Queen's Speech of the twentieth century, in which the words 'modernization', 'new', 'reform' and 'change' were used seventeen times – almost one a minute. Baroness Symons in opening the debate on the Queen's Speech in the House of Lords confirmed that 'We all need to modernize'.

Of the eight chapter headings in the government white paper on House of Lords reform, five contained the word 'modernization'. Labour's move to modernize the House of Lords relied on the assumption that Conservatives would not die in the ditch to defend tradition. On the contrary, Labour reasoned, the party would be obliged to make a grudging retreat before the forces of modernization – to accept, as President Clinton put it, that we must 'make change our friend'. After all, as children learn at their grandmothers' knees, everything is not perfect, the world must move on, nothing is for ever. So no more bowings and doffings, garters and stockings in the House of Lords.

Similarly with devolution, Labour encouraged a 'modern' debate to raise questions over Britain's national identity. They knew this would create unease and uncertainty about what Britain meant or stood for. Accordingly, opinion polls would start to show a splintering sense of identity and a growing allegiance to England, Scotland or Wales. Labour knew this move would strike at the heart of Conservative values, leaving its opponent uncertain about what it thought were settled notions of the United Kingdom and Great Britain.

And, of course, a Britain in bite-size pieces would make a more complicated prelude to Labour's final riddle.

Riddle no. 4: Now vs Never

Chess grandmasters say the game favours the player who can best exploit a situation by sustaining the tension as long as possible.

So Labour declined Brussels' invitation for an early move into a single European currency, preferring a wait-and-see policy. This suited Labour well, because they were not waiting to see how the Euro performed but to see how much pressure the Conservative Party could take before it cracked.

So they wanted to give Conservatives plenty of time to hear all their arguments. Of course, they said, everyone wants to be in charge of their own fate. But nothing is completely sovereign. No man is an island, not even this one.

Dante spelled out Labour's approach 500 years ago. In 1459, he wrote, 'Humankind at its best depends upon unity in the wills of its members. The Scythians, for instance, live outside the Seventh Circle, experience extreme inequalities of day and night, and endure an almost intolerably piercing frost; they require a different rule from the Garamantes who live in the equinoctial zone, where the days and nights are of equal duration and where the excessive heat makes it unbearable to wear clothes. But our meaning is that humankind should be directed by a common law issuing from one supreme prince, and applied to those characteristics which are common to all men.'

So Labour reminded us that, for example, the rule of law required a compulsory jurisdiction, that we had already accepted the degradation of our own sovereignty because foreign judges made decisions that we had to accept as a necessary result of the international rule of law, that the Human Rights Act brought Britain in the first year of the new century within the European Convention on Human Rights.

We were shown how, with global financial markets, economies were interdependent, how environmental problems – the ozone layer, climate change, biodiversity – could not be solved at the national level, how the World Trade Organization could not allow contravention of rules by one country in pursuit of its own sovereignty.

Did this New Labour riddle succeed?

At the end of the twentieth century polls showed that seventy per cent of the British people did not want to join the Euro. This was seen as a triumph for Eurosceptics everywhere. But the same polls also showed that seventy per cent believed we would inevitably join the Euro. Since that figure matched the percentage who know the name of the Prime Minister at any one time, it was the near unanimous view of the British people in the first year of the twenty-first century that Britain would join the Euro. A triumph for Euro fans.

What did those contradictory poll findings mean?

Some said the results showed that the British public was moronic. Because if they did not want the Euro all they had to do was vote against it in a referendum and then it would not happen.

In fact, these findings illustrated how very intelligent the British people were. Because they understood very well that there are certain things in life you don't want, but to which you have to bow your head. They knew you have to bow your head to death, to illness, to failure, or, perhaps, to the march of history. And they may have been reasoning that this Euro was something they didn't want but which they knew they would just have to accept.

In part, they may have been led to this conclusion by the irrationality of some objections to the Euro. Anti-Euro spokesmen at the time provided two sets of reasons to reject the Euro. The first was economic: it would fail; it would cost jobs, raise taxes, lower pensions, etc. Bad things would happen. The second set of reasons was constitutional: to do with sovereignty, our proud traditions, our independent nationhood, etc.

Eurosceptics put forward both these arguments to explain why they wanted to delay entry. The first set of defects – the economic ones – was capable of remedy by delay. In other words, a rational person could say, 'I am a cautious person. I think this will go wrong. I am prudent and therefore I will wait and see. What's the rush?' That is a completely coherent position. And in the event that time passed and those fears proved groundless, then a rational person would say, 'Fine. Now I am satisfied. Now I go in.'

But the problem was that the second set of objections – the constitutional ones – was not capable of remedy by delay. There will never be a time when the arguments about sovereignty can be overcome by observation of economic outcomes. And in the rational world of the British electorate, the public could sense the logical flaw in the political argument.

Those who opposed the Euro often seemed to be engaged in a battle they had already won, to convince the public that they did not want the Euro. But seventy per cent already agreed. So the task was to convince them they didn't *have* to have it. In other words, to answer the simple question, 'How can we make it on our own?'

As usual, a shrewd public was miles ahead of the politicans in rationality. They saw the Euro for what it was, another symbol of global capitalism. They saw mega-mergers and global corporate alliances every day. They saw jobs moving away to wherever it suited global corporations to employ people. If nobody could stop the globalization of companies, could the globalization of countries be far behind? Even the proud London Stock Exchange, the jewel in the crown of Britain's financial services industry, could not resist the pressure.

People didn't need a Professor of Economics from the LSE or a Chancellor of the Exchequer from Westminster to teach them this. They knew it all perfectly well. Because their employers were teaching them every day the meaning of *e pluribus unum*, unity is strength. The strong go forward. The weak go to the wall. Size is everything. Only a few will survive.

Politics follows economics. If companies feel that their employees are safer and better off in a global organization then politicians will follow suit, believing their citizens to be safer and better off in a regional alliance. This, of course, is what political leaders in Euroland argued to great effect in order to give birth to the Euro in the first place. From their perspective it was only misplaced fantasy that led Britain to resist.

Some Eurosceptics pinned their hopes on America coming to our rescue. But deep-down people knew this was a forlorn hope. The last American President of the twentieth century did not mention the word 'Euro' once in any speech he made. American multinational corporations had welcomed the Euro and campaigned for it. Why wouldn't they? It was the last step in integrating their European units – a path they had been following for almost twenty years.

So Labour's last riddle remained unsolved. A solution would come when the anti-Euro bodies, including the Conservative Party, provided the public with the answer to the only question that mattered: how can we make it on our own? As the twenty-first century began, people still needed to be inspired by the country's prospects without the Euro, to have a picture painted for them of a glorious independent future for Britain, a positive, confident vision of a wonderful future outside Euroland.

So it was that, as the twentieth century ended, the Conservative Party had been left flat-footed by the riddles of New Labour: uncertain whether to criticize it for being empty or dangerous, a con-trick or candy floss, a copy of Conservatism, or what. Conservatives could not accept that theirs was the generation of Conservatives whose misfortune it was to coincide with the conversion of their chief opponent from a Marxist/socialist party to a modern social democratic party.

To the Conservative Party of the end of the twentieth century Mr Blair had handed a victory over socialism that would have been unthinkable throughout the whole of that century. Yet when the prize of victory fell into its hands, Conservatives were unsure how to respond. They were mesmerized by New Labour and by the riddle of Conservative identity that Mr Blair had so brilliantly created.

It was best described by John Major: 'You go for a swim in the sea. When you come back a man has taken your clothes. He has put them on. He looks like you. When he talks, he sounds like you. He has taken your identity. But if he is you, who are we?'

Readers will be familiar with many of the failed solutions to the riddles of Conservative identity posed by New Labour. Some said not to worry about New Labour. It's all just style over substance: new clothes, same body. Nothing has really changed. Carry on as before. Others, equally relaxed, said it would be quite sufficient to point out the theft of the clothes and leave the public to draw the conclusion that they would rather have the real thing than an imitation. But others said it was more sinister. It was all a con. Mr Blair was a smiling front-man put up by a socialist conspiracy to mask the beast within.

Just as a century before – when they first confronted their new enemy, socialism – Conservatives were slow to decide about the true identity of their new opponent.

As a result, Labour supporters can look back on the 1997 election as a joy in every detail. In the fifteenth of Butler and Kavanagh's famous Nuffield College histories of British elections since 1945, the authors trace in all its glory Labour's path to power: how Labour leaders analysed 'the formidable list of reasons which had caused the party's long-term decline'; how they started their 'cultivation of the tabloids'; their 'establishment of Excalibur, a computerized database'; their formation of the 'rapid rebuttal unit' in Millbank and the 'task force on the key seats'; the 'daily news management meetings'; the 'weekly election strategy meetings'; and so on.

The rationality of Labour's method chilled the blood of Conservative supporters. For example, while the Conservatives before 1997 were researching a representative cross-section of voters, Labour focused its focus groups on one group only. Labour had worked out that the only people that mattered to them were Conservative voters in 1992 who now intended to vote Labour. All they needed for victory was more of those people. Therefore Labour researchers literally lived with such persons, in their front rooms, in their kitchens. They asked them the same question over and over again: 'Why have you stopped supporting the Conservatives?' They found out everything there was to know about them – what they ate, what they liked, what they watched on TV, how they felt about everything, especially the Tories.

Labour then tailored its 1997 campaign to suit that group. All so disciplined, so co-ordinated, so very sophisticated: for Conservatives the 1997 election was an exquisite torture.

Professors Butler and Kavanagh's *The 1997 Election* is an unremitting account of Conservative failure and Labour success. Conservative deficiencies, errors and failures are laid bare in the most accurate and wounding detail. As the inventor of the concept of electoral 'swing', Professor Butler probably knows more about elections than anyone else in Britain. Butler says that of all his election histories, two stand out as the most interesting: 1959 and 1997.

Before 1959 Conservative propaganda had reached a low point in the 1951 general election. Central Office had printed thousands of copies of a new poster and distributed them all over the country, ready to be posted up. It consisted of a picture of a young man, a middle-class, energetic Tory type, jumping out of bed in the morning, bursting with energy, under the slogan 'Get Up and Go with the Conservatives!' The only problem with it was that the time on the clock on his bedside-table read a quarter to ten. All the posters had to be sent back.

By 1956 things were not much better. Iain Macleod reported to Professor Butler that he had no contact with the rest of his colleagues while he was out on the campaign trail. Butler believes that 1959 was a watershed because in that election the Conservative Party pioneered 'modern' electioneering techniques. That year saw the beginning of serious television coverage, mass advertising, press conferences and private polling, in all of which the Conservative Party was the driving force.

Professor Butler believes that 1997 was a watershed too. But this time the tables had been turned. It was Labour, he says, who 'marked a change in style unmatched in any post-war election ...

An altogether new pitch ... of sophisticated presentation'.

For the unfortunates who actually managed the Conservative campaign, Butler and Kavanagh do show some mercy. The main conclusion of their study is that 'the six weeks of the campaign did not of course decide the outcome'. In adopting that line they were subscribing to a popular route to absolution for Tory participants in the historic débâcle of May 1997. The authors say such persons are excused because the Tory disaster of 1997 was written in the stars. Eighteen years of government meant it was 'time for a change'. Sleaze, splits, the ERM débâcle, broken tax promises, and so on all just added to the predetermined nature of the result.

This determinist conclusion is a reasonable one, based on the telling evidence of the tables provided in the book. The voting intention tables give ample testament to the logic of the authors' thesis. They show the impact of two key events: first, 'the forced exit from the ERM ... seriously compromising the Conservatives' reputation for economic competence'; and then, in July 1994, Tony Blair's accession as Labour leader.

The authors show how the Tory lead over Labour in voting intention fell from +5 points just before the ERM exit to −15 nine months later. They show how it then fell from −15 to −30 immediately after Tony Blair took over as leader in 1994. And how nothing much changed thereafter, confirming their view that the Tory defeat was preordained.

But *is* it true that no amount of scientific campaigning by the Conservative Party could have 'decided the outcome'? Is it, as the authors say, 'doubtful the Conservatives could have done much in the campaign to alter the final result'?

There is one piece of evidence for the contrary view, i.e. that political events, however unpropitious, can be shaped by rational human will. It is contained in the book's reconstruction of the events surrounding ICM's 'rogue' poll of 23 April 1997.

Labour's most ruthless act during the campaign – their claim that 'the Tories will abolish the state pension' – was planned all along by Labour leaders. They called it Plan B. It was launched immediately following the Tories' 'Eurosceptic week', which had seen Mr Heseltine's first outing as a copywriter with the Blair/Kohl puppet advertisement. According to ICM that week saw the Labour lead gradually cut to a mere +5 points.

Immediately following a phone call by the Labour leaders to the *Guardian*'s editor, and the publication by the *Guardian* of the ICM poll, Plan B duly appeared. Plan B was ruthless (some would say shamefully so) but effective. In the days following the pensions attack, partly thanks to the Tories' over-dramatic response, pensions became a salient issue for the first time. And Butler and Kavanagh show how the Conservative Party then 'lost dramatically … as a 14 per cent lead amongst pensioners collapsed to a 25 per cent deficit in a week'.

The striking feature of Plan B is that it was preplanned. Some Tories (as we shall see in the next chapter) like to think that political events are not susceptible to this kind of rational approach. They see their political skill residing in their instinctive, visceral reaction to unforeseeable events.

Labour took a different view. Labour had belatedly discovered the weapon of fear, and intended to use it. Butler and Kavanagh unearthed a revealing Labour internal memo which says, 'the only way that fear of us can truly be defeated is by voters having a greater fear of them. That is the simple blunt truth … this is an essential part of our strategy.'

Two things follow from the writers' analysis of this key moment in the campaign: the Conservatives' brief, faltering run at a Eurosceptic stance had worked; and Labour's preplanned response negated it. In the days after Plan B was put into effect, Labour's overall ICM lead rose from +5 to +10, close to the actual result of +13 points.

The lesson seems to be that, by sheer will, the Conservative Party did reduce the Labour lead from +13 to +5 during the campaign, and by the same means Labour did then increase it back from +5 to +13. These were major movements which encourage the view that everything is possible in politics given a scientific frame of mind and cold determination.

But Conservative critics found much to condemn in Labour's rationalist approach. They said that it reduced politics to just 'listening to what people want and giving it to them'. Unfortunately, when this standard Tory critique of Labour was adopted at a recent Cambridge University debate, one student sharply responded, 'Isn't that a good definition of democracy?'

Tories instinctively recoiled from people who were so calculating in their approach, feeling that they must by definition lack principle and be willing to 'say anything to get elected'. They searched for proof that New Labour was an insincere, unprincipled image-obsessed creation.

However, the reality was much more mundane: that in politics everyone starts by associating their own ascent with the good of their party, and then with the good of their country. In the end, all politicians, Labour and Conservative, achieve a satisfying and wholesome synthesis between their personal desire for advancement and their pastoral desire to serve the nation.

Thus Mr Gould wrote that political campaigns are 'acts of war, but ... acts of principle also', that backing Mr Blair for the leadership was not only because he looked a winner, but because 'Tony was going to be the modernizers' candidate', and that 'reforming tax and spend' was 'not simply a question of election strategy but ... of political principle'. This happy combination of personal desire and electoral efficacy is the motif that ran through every aspect of New Labour. For New Labour, morality and efficacy, means and ends, marched hand in hand, as they had a century before at the birth of the Labour Party.

For Mr Blair's was not the first attempt by Labour leaders to apply a scientific approach to politics. The Labour Party was conceived with such a view of history. Its formative years were driven by the belief that a correct assessment of means and ends would define the true goal and how to achieve it: 'The economical emancipation of the working classes is therefore the great end to which every political movement ought to be subordinate as a means.' So ran the provisional rules of the first International Working Men's Association published in November 1864.

The Working Men's Association was created in St Martin's Hall in London on 28 September 1864. Its rules were adopted in the last week in October of the same year by a group of around twenty long-forgotten men and women. But one man made of this scattered collection of individuals an instrument which altered history. Professor Isaiah Berlin described him:

> Karl Marx lived in London. He was the poverty-stricken chief of a non-existent sect, burrowing away in the British Museum, author of works unfamiliar to professional socialists, let alone to the educated public. The British working-class leaders, such as they were at this time, did not know him well, but some of the more enterprising among them looked on him as a learned revolutionary theorist good at formulating ideas. With his friend Engels he was brought into the movement, played a leading part in its British section, and after years of obscurity finally became a dominating figure on the public stage of European and world history.

The First International, and the Marxist doctrines so strongly represented in its preamble, statutes and rules, impressed themselves on people's imagination and, as Berlin says, 'achieved a concrete influence greater than all the other organized social movements of the time, perhaps greater than occurred since the rise of Christianity against paganism'.

The philosophical root of Marxism is the concept of history as a scientific process. There is a march of progress, a historic inevitability, which it is senseless to criticize and against which we fight to our certain doom. In Marx's writing, only the brightest and most gifted are ever aware of these deeper forces of change. These are Marx's 'world-historical figures', towering over, and contemptuous of, their puny contemporaries.

These omniscient beings, as they contemplate the discomfiture and destruction of the philistines, believe they have some crucial insight into the nature of the universe. Professor Popper described them: 'Whatever is on the side of change is just and wise; whatever is on the other side, on the side of the world that is doomed to destruction by the working of the forces of history, is foolish, ignorant, retrograde, wicked.'

For Mr Blair and his companions in the 1990s, as for Karl Marx a century before, 'the forces of conservatism' were a feeble symbol of a creed no longer relevant to the new realities of their blueprint for a new order. They believed that their own brand of change was the latest and boldest achievement of the human mind, an achievement so staggeringly novel that only a few people were sufficiently advanced to grasp it.

They felt a call to change human affairs, refusing to accept the existing state of things. They were suspicious of anyone who did not share their attitude towards change as a daring and revolutionary challenge to traditional thought. They were attracted by Karl Marx's famous exhortation to activism, 'Philosophers have only interpreted the world; the point however is to change it.'

Marx's ideological achievement was to translate Kafka's sense of dehumanization – vast impersonal institutions, bureaucracies, factories, armies, the horror of ant-hill life – into a plan of action. He provided the disillusioned in all lands with a realistic, rational assessment, such as Machiavelli had provided in his day, of the harsh facts of political life. He gave the workers a scientific way of testing and measuring everything that they were offered.

Marx's theory of class war was built on the concept of 'us' or 'them' and the impossibility of social compromise between one class and another. He condemned the idea of a slow *embourgeoisement* – the gradual acquisition of all the attributes and enjoyments of a bourgeois life by the workers as part of their slowly increasingly prosperity and political strength. Instead, Marx predicted and demanded a radical transformation, one great cleansing act.

Marx saw the bourgeoisie and proletariat as historical categories, due to arise and to vanish at specific historical stages in accordance with a scientific formula. As he saw it, proletarians were a class of persons – workers – who were separated from their tools – their means of production – as well as from their raw materials and their product. These had been taken away from them by the masters – masters whose workers were creatures whose labour power was bought and sold on the market like any other commodity. According to Marx, labour had become mere material to be exploited – a commodity treated 'as if it were a thing, a non-human entity, like wool or leather or a piece of machinery'.

Marx provided the angry, the miserable, the poor, the discontented with a specific enemy – the capitalist exploiters, the bourgeoisie. He proclaimed a holy war which gave the poor and the exploited not only hope, but something specific to do: 'Organization for ruthless war: with the prospect of blood, sweat and tears, of battles, death and perhaps temporary defeats; but, above all, the guarantee of a happy ending to the story'.

Consider some similarities between Marx and Mr Blair's approach. Rationality for both of them lay in understanding oneself, the situation one lives in, its class structure and one's place in it. All other forms of thought, they said, are not rational. They lead to self-deception and frustration. To know what to do one must know what and where one is.

For Marx, the 'facts' are objective entities, out there to be discovered, and acted upon until the final rational order of society is reached and what he called 'prehistory' achieves its ultimate goal. Like Marx, Mr Blair's epoch-making moves were to stake everything on 'the movement of history', to identify its author-ized interpreters and to make absolute demands in its name. Progress is the triumph of a given section of humankind – the proletariat or, in Mr Blair's case, the modernizers – as sole carri-ers of this rational development.

This certainty about ends and means, of course, led Marx's followers, and later Mr Blair's, to be accused of calculating ruth-lessness. The whole purpose of Lenin's, or Mr Blair's, working life was the triumph of the revolution as they conceived it. They both justified every one of the acts considered devious – from Lenin's political tactics at the meetings of the Russian Social Democratic Party to the alleged 'rigging' of elections to the new assemblies of Mr Blair's new Britain – on the grounds of the requirements of their respective revolutionary movements.

We cannot know what the future will hold for Mr Blair, but it is interesting to observe how Marxism acted as its own gravedigger. The more effective the political organization of the workers became, the more concessions they were able to wring from the state, the more they were drawn into the path of peaceful reform, and the more solidarity they inevitably felt with institutions that proved not to be a stone wall but a flexible and concession-minded entity.

Trade union legislation of the late 1860s, and the social legis-lation that followed, made other recipes seem more plausible to Labour leaders than Marxist ones. The most important current in this softer brand of socialism was the Fabian doctrine. The Fabian Society was founded in 1883. Its name recalls a Roman general whose motto was 'Slow but Sure'. Fabians exonerated socialists from the heavy obligation of reading Marx. They preached practical possibilities here and now: municipal social-ism and state control of the conditions of labour. They left the

New Jerusalem alone and sought to impregnate the existing forces of society with collectivist ideals.

The Social Democratic Federation, founded by quasi-Marxist sympathizers like William Morris, soon yielded in influence to the Fabian Society founded by Sidney and Beatrice Webb, Bernard Shaw and other radical intellectuals. The Fabians believed, not in revolution, which under British conditions seemed impractical, but in the gradual increase of state and municipal control over individual enterprise, and in the growing process of collective control by scientific experts over the entire social and economic life of the nation. This doctrine of socialism by gradual permeation of government departments and local and municipal institutions denied the very basis of Marx's socialism, with its stress on the inevitability of class war and revolution, and asserted instead the possibility of piecemeal socialization and nationalization.

The Independent Labour Party, founded in 1893, was more sympathetic to militant Marxism than to the Fabian belief in the 'inevitability of gradualness'. But the trade unions were mainly concerned with the improvement of their members' standards of living. The alliance between trade unionism and socialism in England was an ideological compromise which has lasted to this day, long condemned by faithful Marxists as a betrayal of socialism. It was the Fabians and trade unionists who between them were most instrumental in founding, in 1900, the Labour Representation Committee, from which the British Labour Party developed.

*

Marx had foreseen conditions of mounting monopoly and concentration of the means of production, exchange and distribution, with fewer and fewer capitalists controlling vaster and vaster empires, their number reduced by constant internecine warfare. Any current issue of the *Wall Street Journal* will validate that description. But he miscalculated when he concluded that this increasing concentration would cause the increasing alienation of the proletariat, which would be forged into a disciplined revolutionary force that would eventually rise up and take charge. Marx's basic supposition, that internal competition between capitalists would make them depress wages down to the lowest level, proved untrue. Concessions were made; the capitalists proved good pupils of Maynard Keynes and successfully averted the final crisis that Marx believed to be so near.

Concessions to unions, the radical social legislation carried through by Lloyd George in England and Franklin Roosevelt in the USA, the welfare state, Keynesian and post-Keynesian economic policies, were never allowed for in Marx's prognosis. Marx exaggerated people's ability to solve society's deep problems once and for all by finding a scientific solution, a great all-embracing vision that would consign these problems to what Engels called 'the museum of antiquities'. By the time Sir William Harcourt, himself a lawyer of the old school, startled the House of Commons by saying, 'We are all Socialists now', there were very few true socialists left, and only a small though active body in the British trade union world that wanted to adopt the full programme of Karl Marx.

So it was that socialism was invented in England by Karl Marx and finally made redundant in England by Tony Blair. But Labour's roots in romanticism – its faith in a science of politics – lived on, and perhaps achieved its highest form at the end of the twentieth century under Mr Blair's leadership.

3

Cynics say No

How different were the thoughts in the mind of Michael Oakeshott when he gave the inaugural address on assuming the Professorship of Political Science at the London School of Economics. Like Conservatives before and after him, Oakeshott was cynical of propositions derived from a presumed knowledge of 'scientific truth'. He offered no political system, no doctrine, no grand philosophy. His basic affirmation was that nothing can be said with finality.

'Empirical politics,' Oakeshott declared, 'are the product of a misunderstanding.' He insisted that politics 'could not be the result of intellectual premeditation'. And he elegantly dismissed 'the illusion that in politics there is a destination to be reached' in this famous sentence: 'In political activity, men sail a boundless and bottomless sea. There is neither harbour for shelter nor floor for anchorage, neither starting-place nor appointed destination. The enterprise is to keep afloat on an even keel.'

No scientific instruments are required on Professor Oakeshott's boat because for Conservatives, from Burke to Oakeshott, there is no *idée fixe*. Politics is not goal-oriented, not 'directed towards' something. For them, 'aimlessness' is the pinnacle of Conservative morality.

Where did this unambitious philosophy come from?

Strangely, in the texts that illuminate the thinking behind Conservative success it is hard to find a coherent political philosophy. The history of the Conservative Party does not appear to owe much to the work of famous philosophers.

It seems that the Conservative Party's identity – if it can be established in a unified sense at all – must be found elsewhere than in its doctrines. This is because, since its earliest days, the Conservative Party seems always to have mistrusted theories or blueprints. For Conservatives, reason is a vice, unreason is a virtue. There are no points A and B. There are no means and ends because there are no ends.

Disraeli is said to have concluded advice given to the editor of a new party journal by saying, 'Above all, no programme.' Walter Elliot said in the 1920s that 'Toryism is not and cannot be a creed of logic.' As R. A. Butler saw it, 'Conservatism is no mere collection of catchpenny slogans and ephemeral theories; it is an abiding attitude of mind, a code of values, a way of life.' In the 1950s Quintin Hogg said flatly, 'Conservatives do not believe that there is a science of politics.' And in the 1970s Ian Gilmour declared that whatever else it was Conservatism was 'not an ideology or a doctrine'.

As Professor Kedourie cautiously put it, 'Conservatism follows and does not precede the existence of a Conservative Party. It is a natural attempt by a body with a long continuous existence to articulate and make intelligible to itself its own character.' Conservatives insist on a pejorative use of the term 'ideology' to equate ideological thought with 'dogma', and to contrast it with 'common sense' or 'empirical wisdom'. They dismiss 'abstract debate' as a factor in Conservative politics. Yet even if it is the case that Conservatism is based on 'a distrust of the purely intellectual approach' to politics, the notion of Conservatism as a 'non-ideology' is itself a revealing aspect of the creed.

More perceptive observers have refused to take at face value these standard Conservative protestations of ideological innocence, and have discerned in the mass of Conservative writings, speeches, and actions a set of ideas that constitutes the nucleus of a quite elaborate doctrine. Certain common themes emerge: a sense of religion and divine order coupled with a veneration of

Christian virtues; a rather pessimistic view of human nature combined with caution about utopian and rationalist schemes; a hierarchical conception of society, founded on the family as the basic social unit and on the importance of private property; a sense of Empire, or Commonwealth, or Britain's place in the world; a stress on tradition and experience, and thus on evolutionary change; and the understanding that the realm of politics is essentially limited.

While it may be true that the Conservatives have not produced a plethora of 'great thinkers' and do not habitually refer to a canon of 'great works', Anthony Quinton and others have shown that it is possible to see Conservatism as based on four closely related principles. At the core of Conservatism is the notion of *intellectual imperfection*. Related to but distinct from the idea of moral imperfection (i.e. original sin), the concept of intellectual imperfection rests on the premise that abstract reasoning cannot be trusted as a guide for social and political organization.

Following directly from this notion of intellectual imperfection are the Conservative principles of *traditionalism*, *organicism* and *scepticism*. Traditionalism is a belief in established customs and institutions; and, as its corollary, organicism is a hostility to 'sudden, precipitate and revolutionary change'. Scepticism means that the kind of knowledge needed for the successful management of human affairs is to be found not in the theoretical speculations of isolated thinkers but in the historically accumulated social experience of the community as a whole.

In summary, society's complexities are too great for any short-lived social 'plan' to produce practicable, comprehensive schemes of change. And any change carried out must, in Conservative eyes, be implemented through existing customs and institutions. For Conservatives, 'the real', broadly speaking, is 'the ideal'. Social and political relationships as they exist are regarded as essentially 'natural'. Conservatives are not opposed to social and political change per se, but they contend that such change must be evolutionary and organic.

Apart from these four principles no single unifying idea is to be found in the English Conservative tradition, except perhaps a desire to prevent political and social reform from destroying the balanced constitution which Burke described as the key to the peculiarly English reconciliation of order and liberty. In fact, all of these four themes can be traced back to the writings of Edmund Burke. There we find the origin of intellectual cynicism in Conservative philosophy.

Although Burke's 1790 *Reflections on the Revolution in France*, and his *Thoughts and Details on Scarcity* in 1795 actually pre-dated the widespread use of the term 'Conservative' by around forty years, they can be taken as the intellectual starting-point for the Conservative Party. The central premise of Burke's work is that human faculties are inadequate to the task of comprehending society. From this premise much else follows.

First, he is *anti-intellectual*. Burke rejected any appeal to universally valid moral and political principles. Then he is *anti-romantic*. Burke favoured cold realism over utopian dreaming. You find in his writing a note of caution, of pragmatism, sometimes of self-interest, that strikes coldly on the romantic mind. No romantic would feel at home in Burke's company. And he is *anti-change*, or at least against rapid change. Burke believed that a society can only change healthily in accordance with its acquired and inherited character and at a given rate. The duty of statesmen is to minimize the impact and slow the rate of such change.

According to Burke we should concentrate on 'what is', not on what 'should be'. So, of course, there are limits to what political action can achieve. Which leads him naturally to be *anti-state*, or at least to ascribe to the state the most minimal role. He regarded the economy as a self-regulating mechanism with which it would be dangerous to tamper.

Possession is nine-tenths of Burke's law. Conservative identity only emerges in reaction to an attack on the traditional scheme of things. It is only when some ideal or imagined alternative is set beside it that those loyal to the established state of affairs need to justify their endorsement of it. It was up to others to explain why they wanted radical change.

Burke was ready to admit that the best means of conserving a state or an institution was to effect timely reforms. He was profoundly conscious of what he called 'the great law of change'. He saw the reality of inevitable social change, but did not like it.

Burke took political philosophy to a new level of hard-headed practical realism. One of the central themes in the *Reflections* is the need for government to be consistent with human nature – to recognize that government exists in order to restrain the defects in the human make-up. For example, of the poor he said, 'When they rise to destroy the rich, they act as wisely for their own purposes, as when they burn mills, and throw corn into the river, to make bread cheap.' Of 'the will of the people' he wrote, 'Some decent regulated pre-eminence, some preference given to birth, is neither unnatural, nor unjust, nor impolitic. It is said, that twenty-four millions ought to prevail over two hundred thousand. To men who may reason calmly, it is ridiculous.'

It is easy to see why some people say that Burke laid the foundations for the Tory reputation for hard-heartedness. His indifference to the economic plight of the masses was matched only by his indifference to their political sentiments.

The area of Burke's thought that has drawn most criticism is his belief that the state ought not to interfere in social and economic life. Government regulation might raise wages, he said, but in so doing it would raise prices, lower profits, inhibit production, create unemployment and thus worsen the lot of the poor. The state should not undertake utopian schemes of political reform, and neither was it in the interests of either producers or consumers for the state to carry out experiments in economic intervention. For Burke, the state was primarily concerned with the minimal task of protecting religion, securing the person and property of its members, and generally resolving the few issues that remained outside the self-regulating mechanism of the social order.

Burke's thinking resonates through Conservative history. Consider this definition of Conservatism in a speech made at Edinburgh in December 1875 by the fifteenth Earl of Derby, then Foreign Secretary in Disraeli's government: 'To distrust loud professions and large promises; to place no confidence in theories for the regeneration of mankind, however brilliant and ingenious; to believe only in that improvement which is steady and gradual, and accomplished step by step; not to compare our actual condition with the ideal world which thinkers may have sketched.' Or this in 1885 by the Duke of Cambridge, Queen Victoria's uncle, and the commander of all the British Armed Forces: 'It is said that I am against change. I am not against change. I am in favour of change, when it is necessary. And it is necessary when it is unavoidable.' Or think of Quintin Hogg's anti-intellectualism in the 1950s:

Conservatives offer no utopia at all but something quite modestly better than the present. Of catchwords, slogans, visions, ideal states of society, classless societies, new orders, of all the tinsel and finery with which modern political charlatans charm their jewels from the modern political savage, the Conservative has nothing to offer. He would rather die than sell such trash. The stuff of all such visions political is either illusion (in which case they are to be pitied) or chicanery (in which case they are to be condemned). All the great evils of our time have come from men pretending that good government could offer utopia.

Or Professor Hayek's version: 'Conservatism will never, except in short periods of disillusionment, appeal to the young and all those others who believe that some changes are desirable if this world is to become a better place. A Conservative movement, by its very nature, is bound to be a defender of established privilege.'

Burke certainly bequeathed to the Conservative child a clear sense of identity. But how did such an apparently uninspiring philosophy help the adult Conservative Party to be so successful in the 200 years after Burke's death? And how will it suit the next hundred years?

One hundred years after Burke, at the end of the nineteenth century, the Conservative Party was the party of property, the party of Empire and the party of the Church. It believed in the monarchy, the aristocracy, the army and the land.

But that philosophy had begun to wear thin. By defending liberty within the narrow bounds of a purely political idea of 'balance', Burke had left Conservatism open to the charge of presenting nothing more than a defence of aristocratic privilege and political despotism. Nineteenth-century Conservatism was duly equated with simple resistance, and the party was considered a refuge for reactionaries, the insecure, the selfish, the blinkered and the out-of-date.

Until the 1870s, the Conservatives had been associated with the land. But economic and demographic change, especially migration from rural areas after 1850, shifted the balance of population and ultimately of political representation from the countryside to urban areas. If the Conservative Party had remained the political arm of the landed interest it would have been marginalized. In the last quarter of the nineteenth century the Conservatives reached out to new urban and suburban interests and became the party of property in general.

The difficulty for the 'party of property', however, was that, by the mid 1880s, successive electoral reforms had led to the creation of a mass, unpropertied electorate. The secret ballot

(1872), limits on personal expenditure by candidates (1883) and the impact of redistribution (1885) required a new approach to politics.

The argument by which Disraeli tried to wean English Conservatism from its close association with the landed interest, and identify it with the interest of the nation at large, was never presented in a very coherent or philosophical manner. Disraeli's achievement was in keeping with Conservative principles, i.e. practical rather than theoretical. It amounted to the simple notion that Conservatism should be based on broad popular support rather than on support from any one section of the community.

In the place of 'two nations', composed of the impoverished mass and the new industrial plutocracy, Disraeli's Young England group wanted to put 'one nation', under the leadership of an aristocracy imbued with a sense of its responsibilities to the people at large. Disraeli rewrote British political history as a struggle between a small, propertied party of Whig oligarchs, who were depicted as a class exclusively dedicated to the pursuit of its own sectional interest, and the Tory Party, which always selflessly upheld the best interests of the nation. His distinction between 'class' and 'nation' would make the Tory Party the true representative of the nation as a whole.

This was how Disraeli rescued the Conservative Party from Burke's sceptical and pessimistic outlook. He redirected the party away from Parliament in favour of intuitive leadership in touch with the needs of the masses. In his famous Crystal Palace speech of 1872 he described the 'historic function' of the Conservative Party as 'the elevation of the condition of the people'. It was a revolutionary change of direction that proved critical to Conservative survival.

Disraeli began the painful adaptation of the Conservative Party into its modern form as a predominantly middle-class, suburban, property-owning, low tax and small state party. As one contemporary saw it, 'This is Disraeli's particular value to the Right: he helps the romantic to feel at home in company that might otherwise seem rather hard-headed or unenterprising for his taste.'

But to Conservatives who retained the Tory suspicion of the masses, the new, increasingly extraparliamentary character of politics seemed fraught with danger. To the sceptical mind of Lord Salisbury, for example, the future awaiting British Conservatism looked bleak.

In 1883, Salisbury published an article in the *Quarterly Review* with the simple and graphic title 'Disintegration'. The policy of concession to democracy and social reform, he wrote, would have 'disastrous and irreversible consequences' for the future of British government. It would ensure the end of the mixed constitution that had been the basis of British political life since 1688. The sovereign and the aristocracy would be excluded from their traditional place in the constitution, and effective power would lie solely with the House of Commons, unlimited by any other authority. Since the Commons would increasingly be dominated by men without property, Salisbury said, 'Law and government would increasingly assume a class character, and be directed to the expropriation of the assets of the propertied section of society'.

The 'Hotel Cecil' (as Churchill liked to describe Lord Salisbury's home at Hatfield House) could not be reconciled to the 'preponderance of working men in the constitution'. Salisbury predicted that they would 'act en masse with a success which no class or order of man not bound together by religious ties has ever succeeded in attaining to before. In such a situation the Conservative Party, of course, can have no future'.

In his concern about the growth of trade union power and the possibility of the dispossession of the haves by the have-nots, Salisbury anticipated sentiments that were to become increasingly influential among Conservative intellectuals and others who did not share John Stuart Mill's optimism about the peaceful progress that lay ahead for democracy. The Conservative Party of Lord Salisbury's era foresaw vast social, economic and constitutional problems. They were anxious about Britain's economic position, about the role of the state and welfare provision, about rising trade union militancy and how to respond to it. They were apprehensive about constitutional developments, and paranoid at Britain's decline.

The old laissez-faire doctrine that the state's only function was to keep order had passed away. Undermined in theory by Carlyle, Ruskin and even Mill in his later days, it had proved inadequate in practice. A new age had come in with the new century.

Whatever party or doctrine would be the ultimate gainer, the old forms of militant imperialism and Conservative Unionism were never again to hold power. The Conservatism that came back after the First World War, as an alternative often preferred to Labour governments, was liberal in its outlook and semi-socialist in its conception of the duties of the state to the working-class. As G. M. Trevelyan wrote, 'In future every Government, whether called Conservative, National or Labour, must be at least half socialist.'

In that great transition, the January 1906 general election was a formative moment for the twentieth-century Conservative Party.

In a century of success this is one of the two periods that Conservatives would rather forget.

Soon after their triumph at the 'khaki' election of September 1900, the Conservatives fell into an electoral slump. A series of poor by-election results led up to the 1906 election, in which the Conservative parliamentary contingent was reduced to its lowest-ever level of 157. In the two general elections of 1910 the Conservatives recovered ground, but they remained pinned in opposition by an unprecedentedly cohesive anti-Conservative bloc. When the Great War broke out in 1914 the Conservatives had lost three general elections in a row and had been in opposition for eight years.

The election of fifty-four Labour representatives was bad enough, but between 1906 and 1910 the Liberal Party went on to introduce social reforms for the poor at the expense of the rich, and extended its appeal to the mass electorate in class terms. In the 1880s and 1890s Salisbury's adroit political management had seemed to defend property effectively. But in the early years of the twentieth century confidence in the Salisburyan approach receded.

New research on 'the poor condition of the people' strengthened the belief that mass enfranchisement would result in the secularization and class polarization of politics. A series of investigations of poverty produced alarming results. Charles Booth's and Seebohm Rowntree's studies indicated that almost a third of the population of London's East End and of the city of York were living in poverty. These revelations, coupled with the extension of the franchise to a large section of the poorer classes, propelled social policy towards the centre of English politics. From the early 1880s, the 'condition of the people' was an issue that nobody in public life could avoid.

There were calls for more inquiries into the state of the 'submerged'. From 1884 onwards, commissions on 'sweated trades' and on housing, sometimes with the Prince of Wales as chairman, examined hitherto unplumbed depths of society. As Engels wrote in 1885, 'As to the great mass of the working people, the state of misery and insecurity in which they live now is as low as ever, if not lower. The East End of London is an ever-spreading pool of stagnant misery and desolation, of starvation when out of work, and degradation physical and moral when in work.'

Booth's scientific study of the London poor, poured out in volume after volume over a series of years, informed the world and formed opinion. His analysis, based on the widest and most detailed collection of facts, showed that in 1891 over 1.25 million out of the 4.3 million Londoners habitually fell below the 'poverty-line', with disastrous results to health and industrial efficiency as well as to human happiness. Booth put the call for old-age pensions on to a firm statistical footing.

These fights against sweating, bad housing, neglect of children and the elderly, and all the problems of poverty, attracted the young Winston Churchill. As early as 1899, Churchill, echoing Disraeli, had put 'the improvement of the condition of the British people' in the forefront of his address to the electors at the Oldham by-election. Just before Christmas 1901, Churchill read Seebohm Rowntree's newly published book *Poverty: A Study of Town Life*. Rowntree's analysis impressed the young Tory, and in his 1909 book *The People's Rights* he wrote, 'A certain minimum standard is necessary, if the head of a family is to be able to bring up children who will be valuable citizens of the state and if he is to maintain a decent standard of comfort. Whatever power may be given to us shall be used for this object.'

In that book Churchill praised Disraeli for his policy of health reform. He applauded the Conservative Party, in the elections of 1892 and 1895, for its commitment to extensive social programmes like the Workmen's Compensation Act and old-age pensions. But then he invited his readers to consider the very different Conservative Party of 1909:

Not a single plan of social reform or reconstruction. Upon the grim and sombre problems of the Poor Law they have no policy whatever; upon unemployment no policy whatever; upon the question of the land, monopolized as it is in the hands of so few, denied to so many, no policy whatever. We are not offered an alternative policy of progress, we are not confronted even with a policy of standstill, we are confronted with an organized policy of constructive reaction.

The Conservative Party, he said, was 'sneering at every philan-thropic enthusiasm'. From it, he heard only 'the weak, maudlin whine of selfish riches'.

Churchill's romanticism was more in touch than Conservative cynicism with the mood of the times.

All over Britain the last two decades of the nineteenth century had seen a huge extension of municipal socialism. Baths and wash-houses, museums, public libraries, parks, gardens, open spaces, allotments, lodging-houses for the working-classes were acquired, erected or maintained out of the rates. The self-gov-erning towns of England became employers of labour on a great scale.

In those last twenty years of the century the Independent Labour Party was founded by Keir Hardie. But at the election of 1895 all its twenty-eight candidates for Parliament were defeated, and in the 'khaki' election of 1900 only two were elected. To the very end of Queen Victoria's reign the great work-ing-class constituencies, even the miners, refused to vote Labour. The Labour Party was of little importance when the twentieth century began.

But then came a decision by the House of Lords from which much of our Left/Right political history takes its origin. In the Taff Vale decision of 1901 the law lords ended the trade union rights that had been held for a generation under Gladstone's Trade Union Act of 1871. The decision gave impetus and power to the Labour Party, which was destined in a generation to destroy and replace the Liberal Party.

What was the legal case that had such momentous political consequences for the Conservative Party? Some employees of the Taff Vale Railway Company in South Wales had been guilty of violent conduct during a strike. The railway company was per-suaded by its lawyers, contrary to the usual practice, to sue the

Amalgamated Society of Railway Servants. The case went up to the Court of Appeal in the House of Lords. The law lords decided that the union could be sued in its corporate capacity for damages alleged to have been caused by the action of its officers, and that it could be sued not merely for criminal acts but for acts, not unlawful, that had caused loss to others. The union had to pay £23,000 in damages.

This entirely new and unexpected interpretation of the Act of 1871 by the law lords of 1901 struck at the very heart of trade union action. Under the Taff Vale judgement, trade unions could not, under threat of losing all their funds in damages, take any strike action to raise wages or to prevent the lowering of wages. The great industrial employers, mostly supporters of the Conservative Party, took advantage of this new state of affairs between 1901 and 1906.

Balfour's government tried to assist the new status quo in the customary manner, by appointing a Royal Commission to investigate. Sidney Webb, who sat on the Commission, wrote, 'This Commission, it is believed, was told privately not to report until after the general election, in order that the Conservative government might not be embarrassed by the dilemma.'

It didn't work. The general election of January 1906 proved a catastrophe for Conservatism. In the débâcle, a great part was played by working-class determination to get the Taff Vale decision reversed by legislation, to save the trade union movement and recover the use of the strike weapon in bargaining. One of the posters in that election showed a fierce-looking judge in wig and robes putting a red-hot poker into the hands of an employer to lay on one of his workers. The Labour Party pledged to give trade unions complete immunity from legal proceedings. This time Labour ran fifty candidates and thirty were elected.

So it was that the Labour Party in January 1906 came into parliamentary existence on the floor of the House of Commons and became a third party in the state. Miners, railwaymen and transport workers became organized on a national instead of a local basis.

But to Conservatives they threatened to become 'a state within the state'. So, in 1909, the House of Lords did it again. At the instigation of Conservative leaders, it proceeded to commit 'the greatest error in modern politics'. It threw out Lloyd George's budget.

Lloyd George's budget was unpopular with the upper-class because it proposed new land taxes and introduced a graduated income tax and death duties in order to pay for old-age pensions. The Lords' rejection of the 1909 budget was a new interpretation of the constitutional function of the hereditary chamber in matters of finance. It was seen to amount to a claim by hereditary peers to force a general election whenever they wished. Winston Churchill, campaigning for the Parliament Bill around the country, asked: 'Why should their children govern our children? Why should the sons and the grandsons and the great grandsons have legislative functions?' He hoped the Bill would be 'fatal to the hereditary House of Lords'.

If the peers could throw out a budget, the government could not raise taxes and any Parliament not to the peers' liking could be dissolved at their will. The rejection of the budget was a breach with the custom of the constitution, of which Conservatives were supposed to be the guardians. The hereditary chamber at the beginning of the democratic twentieth century was claiming powers it had not exercised even in the aristocratic eighteenth.

As a result, the Parliament Act of 1911 was passed and would govern Britain's constitution for the rest of the twentieth century. Commending the Parliament Bill to the House of Commons on its Second Reading, the Liberal Prime Minister, Mr Asquith, said: 'Take the hereditary principle. What can we get out of it? Hon. gentlemen opposite have got a great deal out of it … a working instrument to frustrate and nullify the functions of this House when there is a Liberal Government in power …'

The Lords would not amend money bills. The Lords' veto on legislation was reduced to delaying power only.

And the Conservatives lost the moral high ground.

As with its uncertain response to New Labour at the end of the century, Conservative failure at the beginning of the twentieth century stemmed from uncertainty about how to define its new enemy, socialism.

Disraeli's solution had been to connect his new Conservatism with the poorer and more numerous of the 'two nations' into which his youthful vision saw England divided. He had altered the law affecting strikes to assist the working-class and carried out a mild programme of social reform. But his lead had not been followed. Salisbury had no place for such thoughts. Randolph Churchill, Disraeli's spiritual successor, misplayed his hand and disappeared. Balfour, in many respects a reformer, knew little about working-class thought and aspiration.

Many Conservatives had recognized that in a mass, urban society the underprivileged could not adequately be protected from the ravages of social and economic misfortunes by local, voluntary philanthropy. They argued that state intervention was needed to rescue the poor, the weak and the sick, and to provide a wide range of public services including education.

But others were unsure. The Conservative Party became split into paternalist and libertarian camps, as it has remained to this day. The two schools denounced each other as 'un-Conservative' in a century-long dispute about the proper role of the state.

By the 1950s, the tensions were still unresolved. Harold Macmillan has described how he (as Prime Minister) worked on a proposal to create a National Economic Development Council, drawn from trade unions, management and government, to 'participate in central planning advice'. The establishment of this body was ultimately agreed by the Cabinet but only after two long meetings which revealed, Macmillan said, 'A quite deep divergence of view between ministers, really corresponding to whether they had old Whig, liberal, laissez-faire traditions, or were Tory paternalists and not afraid of a little *dirigisme*'. Macmillan wrote in his diary of his bemusement that some of his critics in the party demanded 'more planning', while others urged that the 'liberal economy' had never been 'given a chance'.

Macmillan's 1935 book *The Middle Way* was an attempt to evolve a new type of economic order, an alternative to capitalism or socialism. He believed that existing experiments in planning were piecemeal and partial. He wanted to carry further the idea of planning without drifting into a pale imitation of socialist planning and the extension of state control.

The Conservative search for a new synthesis of capitalist and socialist theory began in earnest after the Second World War and the calamitous election defeat of 1945. The Tory Party conference in Blackpool that year appointed a committee under the chairmanship of R. A. Butler to draw up a Declaration of Economic Policy. 'The Industrial Charter' was published in May 1947, and its purpose was 'to reconcile the need for central direction with the encouragement of individual effort'. It accepted as irreversible the nationalization of coal, the railways and the Bank of England. Its theme was co-operation between government and industry, each playing its proper part, with a new sense of partnership between owners, management and labour.

By 1950, the Conservatives had accepted not only the welfare state but a much broader system of insurance and benefits for old age, illness and unemployment. Under Macmillan these policies were presented as the quintessence of paternalist and Disraelian Conservatism.

At the same time, the anti-socialist theme continued. In the election of 1950 Churchill usually inserted a lengthy anti-socialist tirade into his speeches: 'Beware! For we may be at the parting of the ways. The socialist conception of the all-powerful state entering into the smallest detail of the life and conduct of the individual, and claiming to plan and shape his work and its rewards, is odious and repellent to every friend of freedom. So far we are only at the first stage in this evil journey.'

However, the long-term success of the Conservative Party at the end of the twentieth century only came when it made itself the advocate of free-market capitalism. It began to say that it could manage capitalism more efficiently than Labour, and because it could manage it more efficiently it could manage it more humanely. As Mrs Thatcher put it, 'Caring that works costs cash.'

It was in the 1970s that her claim to a happy combination of economic efficiency and moral superiority became explicit for the first time. Inspired by Friedrich Hayek's *The Road to Serfdom*, Conservatives first argued that personal freedom and democracy thrive best in a climate of competitive capitalism.

In a series of speeches in 1974–5 Sir Keith Joseph first proclaimed what was to become the winning Conservative theme for the rest of the twentieth century. The focus of his 1976 document, 'The Right Approach: A New Start for Britain', was the sorry state of decline into which Britain had fallen. Economics was the priority: 'National solvency is not so much an objective as *conditio sine qua non* for the attainment of any objectives.' Middle-class values were to the fore:

An important element in bourgeois, or what we call middle-class values is a further time-horizon, a willingness to defer gratification, to work hard for years, study, save, look after the family future. By contrast, workers in this country have traditionally tended to spend their money as it comes. This is not a function of income but of class status and traditions; the peasant and small shopkeeper have traditionally shared this emphasis on the future with the better-off members of the middle-class.

A smaller state was required: 'The idea that the government ought to run everything, rather than private individuals or companies, which forms the core of socialism, is not new at all. It means the bureaucratization of society, with the civil service running everything. The government is already far too big.' And Socialism was a dangerous menace: 'I am extremely aware of the dangerous duplicity of socialism, and extremely determined to turn back the tide before it destroys everything we hold dear. The best reply to full-blooded socialism is not milk and water socialism, it is genuine Conservatism. We shall do what we have said we will do – set the people free.'

'The Right Approach' tried to place the new direction for the Conservative Party within the historical and philosophical traditions of British Conservatism. Disraeli would have been proud of the closing lines: 'Conservatives are not egalitarians. We believe in levelling up, in enhancing opportunities, not in levelling down, which dries up the springs of enterprise and endeavour and ultimately means that there are fewer resources for helping the disadvantaged.'

And so began the twenty-year intellectual hegemony of the Conservative Party, triumphantly crowned at the end of the twentieth century when its old adversary made the historic announcement that Labour too would adopt Conservative economics.

In its first hundred years the Conservative Party had fought democracy and reform, before which it eventually succumbed. In its second hundred years it fought socialism, over which it eventually triumphed. But in victory or defeat it knew which war it was in.

Which war should the Conservative Party fight in the twenty-first century?

4

The New Enlightenment

In a remarkable essay in 1708 titled *An Answer to the Question: What is Enlightenment?* Immanuel Kant declared that 'to be civilized is to be grown-up'. To be grown-up, he wrote, is not to abdicate one's responsibilities to others, not to permit oneself to be treated as a child or barter away one's freedom for the sake of security and comfort. He said a paternalist government, based on 'the benevolence of a ruler who treats his subjects as dependent children ... is the greatest conceivable despotism and destroys all freedom'. Unless a creature can determine itself, he said, it is not a moral being. Kant was absolutely definite on this point: autonomy was the basis of all morality.

Kant's political writings were celebrated models of liberal rationalism. He is a symbol of the old Enlightenment of the eighteenth century. Yet his teaching is an appropriate starting-point for the 'New Enlightenment' of the twenty-first century. Like Locke, Rousseau, Jefferson and most of the champions of liberal democracy, Kant placed immense stress on independence, inner-directedness, self-determination. He wanted a free man to be able to say, 'I am the captain of my soul.'

If ever there were a chance to make that dream to come true it will be in this twenty-first century.

At the end of the twentieth century one of the prime influences was Moore's Law, named after the founder of Intel. His Exponential Law of computing stated that the number of components on a computer chip would double every two years (*Table 1*), with a resulting increase in the speed of computing.

Table 1. The Exponential Law of Computing

Year	Transistors in Intel's latest computer chip
1972	3 500
1973	6 000
1978	29 000
1982	134 000
1985	275 000
1989	1 200 000
1993	3 100 000
1995	5 500 000
1997	7 500 000

Experts say that in the twenty-first century genetic engineering, DNA computers, molecular electronics, photonics, and so on will ensure that the Exponential Law continues to apply. By 2009, a $1000 personal computer will perform a trillion calculations per second. By 2019, a $1000 computing device will approximately equal the computational ability of the human brain. And by 2029, a $1000 unit of computation will have the computing capacity of approximately one thousand human brains, and computers will have read all available human- and machine-generated literature and material.

This technology, according to some, has already transformed economics. As the new century began, the chairman of the US Federal Reserve Board hailed advances in technology as the bearers of productivity increases that would enable the US economy to defy previously inviolate economic laws. He said it made the impossible possible: high growth with low inflation, low inflation without high unemployment.

Related to these advances, a New Enlightenment has been declared – a democracy of information, in which the need to know is replaced by the right to know. As the twenty-first century began, the people in Plato's cave woke from their sleep and had a revelation. They realized that information is knowledge, and that knowledge is power. And they asked themselves, why should all this knowledge be shared only among the elite? Why shouldn't it be shared among all the people? Why should the people stay in the dark?

As in Plato's allegory, they wanted to see the light, to let the light shine on the objects, to see the real objects in their true light. So now, as the twenty-first century begins, we know everything. We know how much the Queen earns. We know the pension of the chairman of ICI. We know the marital condition of our movie stars, and the sexual condition of our politicians. We know which schools produce the best A levels, which hospital has the best record for hip replacements, how much tar and nicotine there is in a cigarette, and the precise contents of a packet of cornflakes.

The position is no longer as described by President Nixon. One day in the Oval Office, President Nixon and Secretary Kissinger were discussing a particularly troublesome affair of state. Mr Nixon made a proposal to solve the problem. Mr Kissinger disapproved: 'Mr President, I must remind you of the famous saying, You can fool *all* of the people *some* of the time, and *some* of the people *all* of the time, but you can't fool *all* of the people *all* of the time ...' President Nixon leaned back in his chair, thought carefully for a moment, then said, 'Henry! Those sound like pretty good odds to me ...'

But in the twenty-first century the odds may be against President Nixon. Because in the New Enlightenment it will be impossible to fool *any* of the people *any* of the time. In the twenty-first century people will be so knowledgeable that they will approximate to what economists call the 'perfect market', i.e. perfect knowledge and perfect ability to use it.

In this New Enlightenment, as in the last, people will want

independence, not dependence. They have the knowledge and the desire – what they don't have is the money. That is not just because incomes are too low. It is because even people on low incomes have their already low incomes further reduced by tax. At present, the government first taxes people on low incomes; then it means-tests their incometo satisfy itself that they are in need; then offers them benefits to restore their income back to where it was before they paid the tax; then, finally, it taxes the benefits.

So, at the start of this new century, people's desires and government policies are heading in opposite directions.

Most British governments since the Second World War have been elected on a promise to keep taxes down. Yet most have left office with taxes higher than when they came to power. The tax burden has gone up, whichever party has been in government. So, for fifty years, independence has been eroded.

All governments, whatever their political composition, face budget pressures for better public services. Demands on the public purse tend to rise. Judging from the record so far, the New Labour government has decided to raise tax – just like most previous British governments.

These habitual responses to economic difficulites illustrate the main problems identified in this chapter. Faced with the legitimate need to improve public services and maintain sound public finances, successive British governments, both Labour and Conservative, have chosen to raise the overall burden of taxation. This has been going on for over forty years.

As a result, close to half of the spending decisions that are taken in Britain are taken not by individuals but by the government on their behalf. Yet apart from a small amount of capital income and rent, the government has no money of its own; all the remaining spending has to be paid for by the people. Today, government has to take away almost forty per cent of earnings through a complex range of taxes (*Table 2*). Of course, the government does not just keep this money. It gives it back to people through social security benefits, the provision of national defence, the NHS, the education system, and so on (*Table 3*). Critics have argued endlessly about the rights and wrongs of these expenditures. But what seems to be unarguable is that for every pound spent *by* the government, individuals are dependent *on* the government for that particular item of expenditure.

Table 2. How we are taxed

	£ billion	Share (%)
Personal taxation		
Income tax and capital gains tax	81.8	27.3
Council tax and motor vehicle duty	14.0	4.7
National Insurance contributions	21.5	7.2
Value-added tax	55.6	18.5
Other taxes and duties on products	44.8	14.9
Inheritance tax	1.7	0.6
Total personal taxation	**219.4**	**73.1**
Taxes levied on companies		
Corporation tax	30.4	
Employers' National Insurance contributions	29.6	
Non-domestic rates	14.9	
PRT, utilities windfall tax and other business taxes	5.7	
Total taxes levied on companies	**80.6**	**26.9**
Total personal and company taxation	**300.0**	**100.0**
GDP at current market prices	813.6	
Total taxes as a percentage of GDP	**36.9**	

Source: ONS Financial Statistics, October 1998

Table 3. The structure of government expenditure

	£ billion	Share (%)
Social security and housing benefits, of which:	105.2	32.9
National Insurance benefits and pensions	44.8	14.0
social assistance benefits in cash	60.4	18.9
Education	36.2	11.3
Health	35.3	11.0
Defence	20.9	6.5
Other local government (England)	14.8	4.6
Home Office, Cabinet Office and legal departments	13.3	4.2
Scotland	12.9	4.0
Environment and transport	9.7	3.0
Wales	6.5	2.0
Northern Ireland	5.5	1.7
Trade and Industry; Culture, Media and Sport	4.9	1.5
Agriculture, Fisheries and Food; CAP	4.1	1.3
FCO and International Development	3.3	1.0
Social Security (administration)	3.3	1.0
Net payments to EC institutions	2.1	0.7
Central Government gross debt interest	28.3	8.8
Accounting and other adjustments	13.5	4.2
Total managed expenditure	**319.8**	**100.0**
GDP at current market prices	813.6	
TME as a percentage of GDP	**39.3**	

Source: ONS Financial Statistics, October 1998

It is not as though this steady increase in taxation has achieved a noble purpose. On the contrary, the terrible problem at the heart of the present system has not gone away: taxes always seem to be going up, yet there never seems to be enough money to spend on good things like health and education.

Nor has the political debate moved on. Right-wing politicians have always said that taxes should be cut to increase self-determination, and the only way they could think of to do that was to cut public spending. But the Left always said that tax served a moral purpose, and it would be cruel and uncaring to cut public spending. That was it: stalemate. The tax burden went up, whoever was in office.

The present system of tax and spending is not something that has changed significantly from day to day, year to year, government to government. It is the result of the practices that have been followed, and the institutions that have developed.

King Edward I expressed the original principle of taxation: 'To each his own! We must find out what is ours, and due to us. And others, what is theirs, and due to them.' From the earliest times, governments have imposed taxes in order to finance military expenditures. Income tax was announced in 1798, and introduced just over 200 years ago in 1799, as a means of paying for the war against Napoleon. William Pitt the Younger was Prime Minister and Chancellor of the Exchequer, and needed greater 'aid and contribution for the prosecution of the war'. 'Certain duties upon income', as outlined in the Act of 1799, were to be the temporary solution. Income tax was to be applied at a rate of ten per cent on the total income of the taxpayer. A short-lived peace treaty with Napoleon allowed Henry Addington, Pitt's successor, to repeal income tax. However, renewed fighting led to Addington's 1803 Act which set the pattern for income tax today.

The 1803 Act looked for a 'contribution of the profits arising from property, professions, trades and offices' (the words

'income tax' were deliberately avoided). It introduced two significant changes: taxation at source, whereby the Bank of England
would deduct income tax when paying interest to holders of
gilts, for example; and the division of income taxes into five
'schedules' designated A (income from land and buildings), B
(farming profits), C (public annuities), D (self-employment and
other items not covered by A, B, C or E), and E (salaries, annuities and pensions).

Income tax changed little under various Chancellors, con-
tributing to the war effort up to the Battle of Waterloo in 1815.
The following year, income tax was abolished and Parliament
decided that all documents relating to it should be pulped.
However, by 1842, the Treasury's coffers were depleted once
more and income tax was revived. There followed a long list of
Prime Ministers who vowed to abolish it, but none of them succeeded. Between the Crimean War and the Great Depression of
the 1880s, income tax receded in significance, supplying only £6
million of the government's £77 million revenue in 1874.
Customs and excise duties contributed the largest share of tax
revenue, at £47 million.

With the formation of a new government by the Liberals following the 1905 election came a change in the way taxation was
viewed, from being a means of paying for wars to a way of supporting the welfare of the people. The structural dependence on
the taxation of personal income and expenditure that is evident
in today's fiscal system was already in place by 1908. The main
development during the past eighty years has been the shift from
the taxation of personal wealth to the taxation of corporate
incomes (*Table 4*).

In 1908, the Chancellor of the Exchequer, Lloyd George, introduced non-contributory old-age pensions, and – in the 'People's
Budget' of 1909 – plans for a tax based on property values. As we
saw in Chapter Three, the rejection of this bill by the House of
Lords led to the 1911 Parliament Act which removed the Lords'

power of veto over money bills. By 1914, the standard rate of income tax was six per cent, and the amount raised from income tax and super-tax was £47 million. By 1918, again to pay for war, the standard rate had jumped to thirty per cent, realizing £294 million per year including super-tax (although tax allowances had also been increased in order to ease the burden for those on low incomes). In addition, an excess profits duty was introduced as a device to deny companies the opportunity to derive exceptional profits from the war effort. At that time, corporate taxation was not normally a significant source of revenue for the Exchequer and it did not become so again until the 1960s.

Learning from the lessons of 1914, the outbreak of the Second World War saw immediate action to raise revenue for the war effort. 'Finance is the fourth arm of defence,' said Chancellor Sir John Simon in the first war budget. In 1939, the standard rate of income tax was twenty-nine per cent with surtax at forty-one per cent. Ten million people were liable for tax, and the total sum raised was £400 million. By 1944–5, successive increases in rates and lowering of allowances meant there were fourteen million taxpayers and nearly £1400 million raised.

The fifty or so years since the end of the Second World War have seen greater social and economic changes than any comparable period. The National Health Service was introduced in 1948. The phrase 'welfare state' began to be used to reflect a wide range of social provisions, including broader National Insurance provisions, the introduction of child allowances, the raising of the school-leaving age and increased old-age pensions.

From 1945 to 1965, the UK economy enjoyed a virtually uninterrupted increase in gross domestic product (GDP) per head, spurred initially by the reconstruction of towns and cities devastated by war. During this time, many industries were under public ownership and control, and roughly twenty per cent of government expenditure was on capital investment. Once the war had ceased to absorb additional resources, the government's

Table 4. Long-term development of the UK tax structure 1908–98

Year	Total tax take	Income taxes on individuals (£ million)	%	Expenditure taxes (£ million)	%	Company taxes (£ million)	%	Wealth taxes on individuals (£ million)	%
1908–9	127	34	26.8	65	49.6	2	1.6	26	20.5
1918–19	786	294	37.5	162	20.7	287	36.6	43	5.5
1928–29	664	293	44.1	257	38.7	3	0.5	111	16.7
1938–39	898	399	44.5	377	42.1	24	2.7	98	10.9
1948–49	3,665	1,460	39.8	1,610	43.9	360	9.8	235	6.4
1958–59	5,310	2,484	46.7	2,298	43.2	275	5.2	253	4.8
1968–69	12,903	4,574	35.5	4,994	38.7	2,782	21.6	553	4.3
1978–79	40,916	18,763	45.8	14,948	36.5	6,050	12.9	1,155	2.8
1988–89	121,382	43,433	35.8	52,376	43.2	19,925	16.4	5,649	4.7
1998–99	226,300	84,300	37.3	100,200	44.3	33,100	14.6	8,700	3.8

Source: Inland Revenue Statistics 1998

current expenditures fell back to around thirty per cent of GDP. The low rate of unemployment and the relatively small proportion of old-age pensioners helped to keep down the cost of National Insurance and other benefits.

In 1948–9, the total of all social security benefits was £471 million, representing under four per cent of GDP. Retirement pensions, war pensions and widows' benefits amounted to £278 million, assistance to families £60 million, benefits to the unemployed and needy £78 million, to the sick and disabled £44 million, and all other benefits £11 million. By 1965–6, social security benefits had already assumed greater importance, at 6.3 per cent of GDP, but pensions and widows' benefits still accounted for almost two-thirds of the total. This share had fallen to thirty-six per cent by 1994–5 as unemployment, invalidity and housing benefits rose to prominence.

Figure 1 shows that 1976–7 was the climax for the share of total government spending in the economy; very nearly fifty per cent of national expenditure was under the direction of the public sector. Strenuous efforts to scale back the influence of government during the late 1970s, prompted by the IMF's intervention in 1976, were frustrated by the slide into economic recession during 1980. Nevertheless, a significant reduction in the size of the public sector occurred in the second half of the decade. Its share of total managed expenditure fell below forty per cent and has returned to this level again in recent years. However, almost all of this is current expenditure; after the large-scale privatizations of the 1980s and 1990s, net investment by the public sector is minimal.

The composition of public expenditure between the various departments and agencies has altered most in respect of social security payments. *Figure 2* illustrates the transformation of their share from twenty per cent in 1970–71 to about thirty-six per cent today. By contrast, expenditures on health and education have changed little during the last twenty years. These budg-

Figure 1. Government spending as a percentage of the size of the economy

Sources: Comprehensive Spending Review, Cm 4011, July 1988 and Pre-Budget Report, Cm 4076, November 1998.

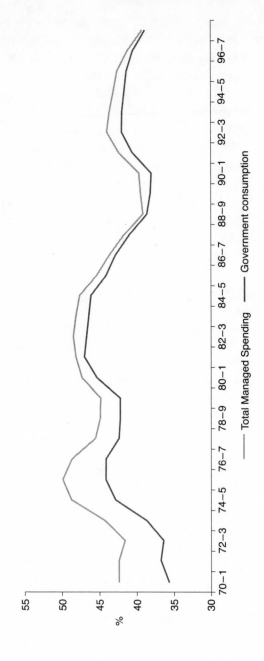

—— Total Managed Spending —— Government consumption

Figure 2. Social security payments as a share of total government expenditure

Source: Datastream.

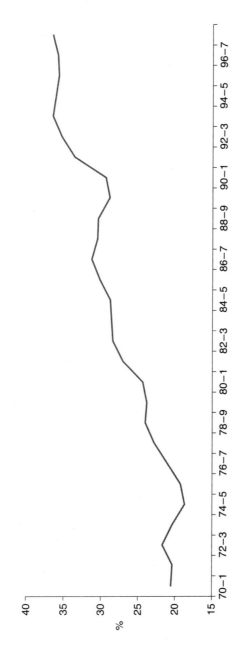

ets have increased in real terms but very little in relation to the total government budget (*Figure 3*).

During the 1950s and 1960s, the UK government's budget was broadly balanced. Tax revenue and other recurrent income (such as rents and surpluses) was sufficient to cover all expenditures, averaged out over a period of five or ten years. In contrast, deficits averaged 2–2.5 per cent of GDP throughout the 1970s and 1980s, only to explode in the aftermath of the recession of the 1990s to 7.8 per cent of GDP in 1993. Since then, the budget has been brought under control and the 1998–9 fiscal year yielded a small surplus. However, vast public debts have been accumulated in the last thirty years and these must still be serviced. Debt interest currently absorbs about 3.5 per cent of GDP, equivalent to eight per cent of all government spending.

It is important to appreciate that the expansion of government, and the associated tax burden required to finance it, has been even more obvious in other developed countries than in the UK. The Organization for Economic Cooperation and Development's Revenue Statistics cover the period from 1965 to 1995, during which the average ratio of tax revenue to GDP has risen from 26.1 to 37.4 per cent (*Figure 4*). For the UK, the growth was from 30.4 to 35.3 per cent over the same period. The most extreme example is Sweden, whose ratio climbed from thirty-five per cent in 1965 to a peak of 55.6 per cent in 1990, before falling back to 49.7 per cent in 1995. Other countries have resisted the trend towards larger government more successfully: the USA's ratio rose only from 24.3 to 27.9 per cent over the thirty-year period.

While there are too many variables to rely on such cross-border comparisons, the dynamic effect of a low tax burden on an economy is illustrated by the USA. The US government taxes only 27.9 per cent of national income. But instead of finding this insufficient to meet its spending needs, it is expected that the US economy will generate an extraordinary budget *surplus* over the next ten years of $2,500 billion.

Figure 3. Share of health and education spending in total UK government expenditure
Source: Datastream.

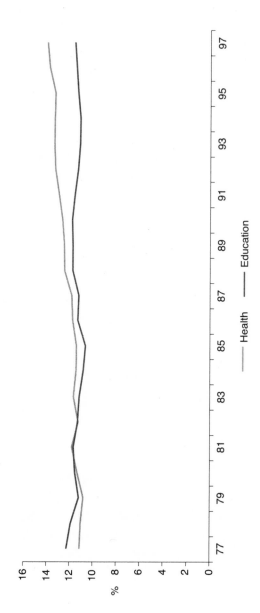

Figure 4. Tax as a percentage of GDP
Source: OECD Revenue Statistics, 1997 edn.

Figure 5. Comparative taxation trends in the EU and the UK

Sources: OECD Revenue Statistics, 1997 edn and Financial Statement and Budget Report, March 1998.

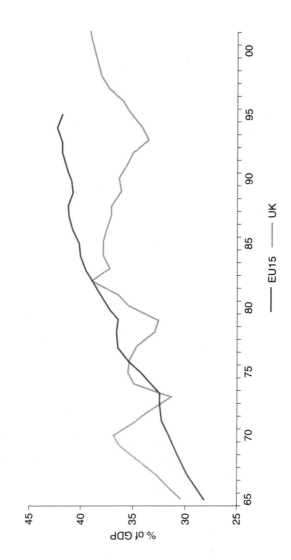

By contrast, consider the tax and spending position in other European Union member states. In 1995, when Britain's tax burden was still 35.3 per cent, the EU average was 41.8 per cent, with Germany at 39.2 per cent, France at 44.5 per cent and Denmark at 51.3 per cent (*Figure 5*).

There was a time when Britain matched the performance of the USA. Between 1955 and 1964, the total UK tax burden averaged 29.3 per cent of the money value of GDP, with little variation from year to year. As *Table 5* shows, this was no flash in the pan; it was achieved over a ten-year period, equivalent to two complete business cycles. At that time, the government's current income from taxation was more than sufficient to cover its current expenditure on goods and services, social security, pensions and benefits.

Table 5. UK tax burden in the last forty years

Year	Total taxation & NICs £ million	Nominal GDP £ million	Tax burden %
1948	4,170	11,835	35.2
	4,474	12,565	35.6
1950	4,501	13,112	34.3
	4,836	14,612	33.1
1952	5,094	15,764	32.3
	5,164	16,906	30.5
1954	5,355	17,890	29.9
	5,735	19,304	29.7
1956	5,983	20,766	28.8
	6,373	21,920	29.1
1958	6,786	22,853	29.7
	7,044	24,213	29.1
1960	7,242	25,887	28.0
	8,024	27,432	29.3
1962	8,784	28,812	30.5
	9,008	30,856	29.2

Table 5 contd

1964	9,762	33,435	29.2
	10,996	36,035	30.5
1966	12,086	38,370	31.5
	13,500	40,400	33.4
1968	15,226	43,808	34.8
	17,105	47,153	36.3
1970	19,220	52,370	36.7
	20,461	58,294	35.1
1972	21,826	66,747	32.7
	25,011	74,661	33.5
1974	32,214	89,733	35.9
	40,374	111,222	36.3
1976	46,606	130,185	35.8
	52,470	151,648	34.6
1978	59,018	174,610	33.8
	73,150	209,598	34.9
1980	85,870	237,209	36.2
	101,270	259,667	39.0
1982	109,467	284,330	38.5
	117,843	308,489	38.2
1984	127,440	331,875	38.4
	138,333	364,035	38.0
1986	148,516	394,989	37.6
	162,135	434,679	37.3
1988	177,616	482,653	36.8
	192,675	525,000	36.7
1990	205,548	566,247	36.3
	205,297	578,302	35.5
1992	205,935	609,276	33.8
	214,889	643,379	33.4
1994	234,524	681,755	34.4
	254,996	720,327	35.4
1996	269,262	760,628	35.4
	293,958	807,576	36.4
1998	318,060	855,000	37.2

Sources: Inland Revenue Statistics and the Pre-Budget Report, November 1998

For a variety of reasons, Harold Wilson's Labour governments of 1964–70 intervened heavily in the economy, raising tax revenues to match substantial increases in public spending. By 1970, the tax take had risen to almost 37 per cent of GDP. Since then, five Conservative governments have worked hard to undo this expansion of public sector influence. But the sustained efforts of the Thatcher and Major administrations did not succeed. In fact, the overall tax burden in 1998 was again over 37 per cent of GDP.

By 2002, Labour's plans are expected to carry the total tax take above 39 per cent, which would represent a peacetime peak. Despite this record increase in taxation, official forecasts show that even then the government's current income will not match its current expenditure. The government will again have to borrow to meet its spending requirements, and the public will again have to accept the familiar combination of high taxes and inadequate public services.

And in the new century, governments will find it harder to raise tax in the traditional way, for a variety of reasons:

e-commerce makes the tax base less clear;

excise duties on tobacco and alcohol have passed their optimal points and begun to generate diminishing returns;

duty on fuel has reached a peak – as shown by the revolts against the Tory extension of VAT to domestic fuel and increases in petrol tax initiated by the Tories and continued under Labour;

political objections make it hard to raise income tax rates;

nobody wants VAT to be raised or extended in scope;

and the way government has found around these difficulties – cutting visible taxes on voters while raising invisible taxes ('stealth taxes') elsewhere – has been exposed and discredited.

Britain's system of tax and spending is an ungainly beast

designed by a committee which has been in standing session for 200 years. The sterile debate on tax and spending is unsuited to a New Enlightenment. It is time time for a change – for a grown-up conversation between government and citizen.

Government: Come on, what's up? You don't seem happy.

Citizen: I'm not happy. I have money worries.

Government: You have money worries. How do you think I feel? I give you a strong economy, millions of new jobs so you can afford cars and TVs and computers and holidays in Florida and still you complain, making me spend all my money on benefits for you … I mean, what do you think I am, made of money? Where's it going to end? I just can't keep going on like this. Don't talk to me about money worries.

Citizen: Who else can I talk to? You're the government, you're in charge.

Government: I know, and I've had enough of your endless moaning and whingeing. Leave me out of it; just talk to an independent financial adviser or something.

Citizen: But I'm not independent, that's the point. What's the use of an independent financial adviser? I have real issues here. What about health care and my parents' old age? What about the kids' university fees? And what about the mortgage if taxes keep going up? And I don't even want to think about the pension and whether that'll be worth anything by the time I retire. I'm genuinely worried and I don't know what to do.

Government: How many times have I told you, you don't have to do anything, I'll take care of all that for you. You worry too much. Relax, I've got it all under control.

Citizen: That's the problem, that's exactly the problem. How do I know it's going to be OK unless I'm in control?

Government: It's going to be OK precisely because you're not in control. Imagine if everybody was in control of their own little lives! Then where would we be? Chaos! Anyway, you couldn't possibly afford to look after all these things for yourself. Have you any idea how expensive health care is? And all these benefit payments I hand out? Where would you get the money?

Citizen: The same place you get it. From me.

Government: What do you mean, 'from me'?

Citizen: Well that is where you get your money isn't it? The only place you can get it. From me.

Government: OK, OK, but I always give it back.

Citizen: I know, so why take it in the first place?

Government: Well, because … because that's how it works. That's the way I've always done it. No one's complained before.

Citizen: Oh come off it, everyone's always complaining. And anyway, I thought you believed in doing things differently from in the past?

Government: I do.

Citizen: So don't take so much of my money in taxes.

Government: But then, how could I afford to pay for all the things you say you're worried about?

Citizen: You wouldn't have to. If you didn't tax me so much, you wouldn't have to pay me so much in benefits. I'd have the money to pay for things myself, which is what I asked for in the first place: a bit of independence.

Government: So you don't mind looking after yourself?

Citizen: No! Not if you don't take so much of my money in tax. Then I could pay for things myself, and you could concentrate on doing the things people really can't do for themselves.

Government: And then I won't have you complaining the whole time?

Citizen: Exactly.

Government: Sounds good to me.

Citizen: Me too. Thank you and goodbye.

The need for such a conversation is evident from examination of the present system.

First, there is now a massive overlap between tax and benefit payments. Every year, the government collects around £30 billion in income tax and National Insurance contributions from 17 million households, to which it also distributes around £30 billion in benefits. So, bizarrely, Britain's tax and benefit system today needlessly transfers £30 billion each year (between nine and twelve per cent of all government spending) in and out of the very same households because of the overlap between taxpayers and recipients of state-administered benefits and pensions.

Last year, the number of individual income tax payers rose to 26.1 million (more than ever before). Tens of millions of benefit claims are paid each week, many of which are income top-ups and housing subsidies to tax-paying working households. How much better would it be if those households simply retained a larger proportion of their earned income. Higher net incomes decrease the need for government benefit payments. The motivation for millions of minor tax and benefit transfers would simply disappear. Without detracting from the overall generosity of the welfare system, the cancellation of overlapping payments would set Britain on a different path.

The extensive and complex system of tax and spending has brought many material advantages to the people of Britain. It has also created some damaging anomalies. Remember that the government spends almost forty per cent of national income. Bear in mind also that roughly one-third of this spending goes on social security benefits of one kind or another. Then consider:

the national average income for a man in full-time employment is £21,600 per annum;

yet 4.4 million people who have total incomes of under £5000
per annum still pay tax;

another 3.6 million taxpayers have total incomes of between
£5000 and £7500 per annum;

another 6.2 million taxpayers have total incomes of between
£7500 and £10,000 per annum;

at the same time, the great majority of these 14.2 million people – all of whom pay tax to the government – also receive
means-tested benefits from the government; many of these
benefits are themselves then taxed.

*Second, there is a bizarre range of methods by which benefits are
assessed for tax.* Some benefits are means-tested in relation to
income; some are means-tested in relation to capital; others are
not means-tested at all. Income tax is based on the income of the
individual, while benefits are based on the income and capital of
household units, defined as individuals living in the same
accommodation and sharing at least one meal together each day.

One result of these anomalies is that the earnings of a single
mother will more than double if she works sixteen as opposed to
fifteen hours per week, and will fall if she works twenty-seven as
opposed to twenty-six hours per week. Another is that a family
with total earnings of £100,000 per annum pays zero per cent tax
on child benefit, but an unemployed household pays tax at one
hundred per cent. For those working sixteen hours per week or
more, child benefit is taxed at sixty-five per cent when assessing
housing benefit and twenty per cent for the calculation of council tax benefit. This is because it forms part of the income calculation that triggers a tapered restriction on these benefits when
resources exceed the relevant thresholds.

The interaction of all these various benefits and taxes creates
a marginal tax rate of ninety-five per cent for hundreds of thousands of households. And capital means-testing for the working
families tax credit means households with savings are heavily

penalized if they confess to holding them in deposit accounts.

Oh what a tangled web!

Third, there has been a staggering proliferation of tax rates. The UK, in common with many other countries, has an extensive array of tax exemptions, special allowances and reliefs (see Appendix 3). While the tax burden is constantly rising, the tax system itself is getting more complicated. And this complexity increases the tax burden further by adding to the cost of administration (see Appendix 5).

According to the latest figures from the House of Commons Library, the number of basic tax rates has more than doubled, from fifteen to thirty-eight, under the present government. *Tolley's Standard Tax Manual*, the bible of tax accountants, has increased from 2529 to 3293 pages. The Finance Bill has reached a record 570 pages in two volumes, taking existing tax legislation to over 6000 pages. The government's last autumn budget ran to 205 pages, plus a further 140 in supporting documents from the Treasury and another 126 from the Department of Social Security.

The Institute of Chartered Accountants recently warned that the tax system was so complicated that it had 'spun out of democratic control'. The Institute for Fiscal Studies says it is now 'extremely difficult' for people to calculate how much tax they are due to pay. There is a mass of over 250 complex tax allowances, reliefs, exemptions, credits, indexations, tapers, disregards and so on that taxpayers have to navigate (see Appendix 3).

For pensioners to claim the government's new minimum income guarantee, for example, requires the completion of a thirty-page application form. Age Concern said the last budget would 'add another layer of complication to an already complicated system'. No wonder that of the 750,000 pensioners entitled to this allowance only 25,000 claimed it.

Some of these allowances are designed to promote pensions,

savings and investment, some to shield expenditures on food and clothing, some to make home ownership more affordable and others to favour small businesses. However, the more complicated the structure of taxation, the greater are its likely adverse side-effects. In addition, the greater the value of allowances and other concessions, the larger the gross (or notional) tax system that is required to raise a particular amount of net revenue.

In 1997–8 the unrelieved taxable potential of the present tax structure levied by the Exchequer on companies and individuals amounted to £434.9 billion. But £134.9 billion, almost a third of the total, was given back in the form of reliefs and allowances. *Table 6* provides some approximate calculations of the size of the gross tax structure as it stood in the 1997–8 fiscal year. If it were unrelieved by allowances and exemptions, the present structure would be capable of collecting tax revenues equivalent to around fifty-three per cent of national income. Through the gradual erosion of allowances, a UK government could achieve EU average levels of taxation almost imperceptibly, which is exactly what has been happening. When the present government came to power there was a six per cent tax gap between Britain and Euroland – in Britain's favour. Today, it is two per cent.

The result of complexity is lack of transparency. The concept of 'stealth tax' is well known – a new tax in a disguised form. But the current system has spawned an even more effective form of taxation hidden in the morass. Economists call it fiscal drag. It means that unless Chancellors of the Exchequer are saints and actively go out of their way to avoid it, tax receipts will automatically grow faster than the economy.

Most people believe the tax system now takes around thirty-eight per cent of GDP. But, as *Table 6* shows, that is just the net effect of the system; the gross system collects a staggering fifty-three per cent of GDP. The citizen is then obliged to claim back fifteen per cent of GDP – £150 billion – in over 250 complex

Table 6. Structure of the UK taxation system (1997–8)

	Tax paid £ billion	Estimated value of tax reliefs £ billion	Notional taxation £ billion
Taxation			
Income tax, capital gains tax & inheritance tax	83.5	63.6	147.1
Council tax and motor vehicle duty	14.0	7.3	21.3
National Insurance contributions	21.5	10.3	31.8
VAT	55.6	28.5	84.1
Other taxes and duties on products	44.8	0.0	44.8
Taxes levied on companies	80.6	25.2	105.8
Totals	**300.0**	**134.9**	**434.9**
Total tax as a percentage of GDP at market prices	36.9%	16.6%	53.5%
Principal tax reliefs			
Personal income tax thresholds		29.6	
Zero-rated VAT items		20.6	
Occupational and personal pension relief		19.2	
Capital investment allowances (companies)		17.1	
Other income tax allowances		16.2	
Exemptions from VAT		8.0	
Other corporation tax and PRT reliefs		8.0	
Inheritance tax and stamp duty reliefs		7.3	
Capital gains tax relief		6.2	
Other National Insurance reliefs		2.7	
Total		**134.9**	

Sources: HM Treasury Tax Ready Reckoner and Reliefs, December 1997; ONS Financial Statistics Table S30, October 1998.

allowances, exemptions and so on. This process gives the government a much greater hold over individuals' lives than it needs, just to achieve the same result.

The charm of such a large gross tax system – from the government's point of view – is the scope it allows for hidden tax increases via reduced allowances. Under this structure, a Chancellor can increase tax without ever announcing a tax rise; Chancellors, being human, have not resisted the temptation, with the result that tax as a percentage of GDP creeps up invisibly, with little political impact. 'Invisible' tax increases, by definition, are not seen – and not being seen, are not felt. People just wake up one morning and find themselves in a higher tax bracket. For example, recent budget changes to income tax rates (the 10p starting rate and the 22p band) were dealt with in two lines, whereas another forty-two lines were required to explain changes to allowances, reliefs and exemptions.

So, despite the new 10p tax band, the personal income tax burden actually increased due to the erosion of the real value of tax allowances, i.e. allowances growing more slowly than earnings, leaving a rising share of personal income liable to tax. That is how the UK's so-called 'strong public finances' have come about – not because of a strong economy (trend growth at 2.25 per cent per annum is lower than that of Euroland and less than half that of the USA), but because of bouyant tax receipts, growing by six per cent this year, the third year in a row in which tax receipts have risen by more than double the growth in GDP.

As a consequence of the erosion of the real value of income tax allowances, millions of low-paid and benefit-dependent individuals are also taxpayers. The extreme disincentives attaching to paid employment arise from the overlapping of low entry thresholds for tax and National Insurance contributions with high marginal rates of withdrawal of social security benefits and privileges. The present system of housing benefits is a particular source of aggravation in this regard. The solutions presented in the 1998 and 1999 budgets (including the reform of National Insurance contributions, the working families tax credit and the forthcoming children's tax credit) point in the right direction but are too small to have a worthwhile impact.

The rise in the tax burden has been accompanied by widening income inequality in the adult population. According to a Department of Social Security study published in 1997, the lower half of the income distribution received thirty-three per cent of total personal income in 1979 and twenty-eight per cent in 1994–5. The top ten per cent of the income distribution received twenty-one per cent of the total in 1979 and twenty-six per cent in 1994–5. Whatever result the increase in transfer payments was intended to achieve, it appears to have reinforced income inequality rather than the opposite.

Part of the explanation for this lies in the fact that wealthier individuals are able to structure their financial affairs so as to benefit from the vast array of exemptions and allowances. For example, in 1995 the £9.3 billion of tax relief for occupational pension contributions was distributed as follows: 2.3 per cent to the poorest quintile of taxpayers; 5.3 per cent to the second-lowest quintile; 9.5 per cent to the middle quintile; 15.7 per cent to the second-highest quintile; and 67.2 per cent to the top quintile. Other examples of tax breaks that accrue disproportionately to the higher income groups are personal pension contributions, TESSAs and PEPs (now succeeded by Individual Savings Accounts or ISAs), mortgage interest relief (soon to disappear) and expenditures, through trusts, on private education. Naturally, those with the largest potential tax liabilities make the greatest effort to discover legitimate ways of sheltering their income from taxation.

The present system provides an incentive for small businesses to operate outside the tax system. The size of the hidden, or 'black', economy in the UK has been estimated by Dr Bhattacharyya of the University of Leicester to have grown to between seven and ten per cent of recorded GDP (equivalent to £57–80 billion for 1997–8). This implies a range for lost tax receipts of £20–28 billion, assuming a thirty-five per cent average tax take on hidden earnings.

Professor Kent Matthews of Cardiff Business School has identified a number of industries, such as restaurants, furniture and floor-coverings, and hairdressing, in which actual VAT receipts fall well short of their predicted levels. The combination of a high VAT rate (17.5 per cent) and a low registration threshold appears to have persuaded thousands of small businesses to operate outside the tax system. In a separate research study, Kent Matthews presented evidence to suggest that some EU countries have already raised their VAT rates to the point where the marginal tax take is actually declining, thereby reducing the public funds available for the health and education budgets.

Britain now has proportionately more households with children without a wage-earner than any other country in the developed world: almost one household in five (Figure 6). Yet twenty years ago fewer than one UK household in ten was workless. This has brought about a remorseless increase, in communities all over Britain, of the linked problems that are now commonly described as 'social exclusion': poor housing, poor public health, low standards of education and high rates of crime. The tax and benefit system is supposed to make things better through the redistribution of income and wealth. But instead it is making things worse by reinforcing the very conditions that lead to social exclusion. At the same time, we are paying more tax than at any point in our peacetime history, a situation that in itself inhibits the economic growth and job creation that could form part of the solution to the problems of social exclusion.

Figure 6. Workless household rate by country for households with children, 1996

Source: Employment Policy Institute Employment Audit Issue 9, Autumn 1998.

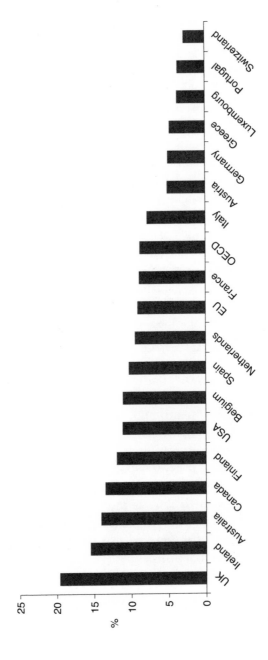

Britain has an ever-increasing tax burden yet struggles to make adequate resources available to public health or education. If opinion polls are any guide, there is enormous public support for the reallocation of government expenditure towards front-line healthcare and primary and secondary education. Yet this transformation has proved elusive even for a government with a massive parliamentary majority.

Incremental reform of the existing tax, National Insurance and benefit system over the last thirty years has created a highly complex and contradictory framework of transfer payments. All attempts to unravel the wasteful and unintended features of the transfer system, such as the unemployment and poverty traps, have been half-hearted and piecemeal. At the start of the twenty-first century, the problems loom as large as ever, and the human and financial costs of large-scale benefit dependency are still escalating.

Attempts at tinkering with the tax and benefit system, rather than redesigning it, have failed. Incremental and piecemeal reform has been the enemy of the best intentions, on all sides. While small steps have been taken in the right direction, the fundamental issues have not been addressed. To break free, the system must be redesigned in the interests of promoting economic growth and employment prospects over the long term.

Calls for modernization are not new. So the question that arises is, why has it never happened? There is one simple explanation. It is not because political leaders are oblivious to it. On the contrary, there is almost universal agreement about what the problems are and the urgency of tackling them. Rather, a national culture has emerged that stops political leaders taking the required action. British politicians have become paralysed by fear of public reaction to fundamental reform of our system of tax and benefits. Every action that is proposed is analysed in terms of winners and losers, short-term effects, precise calculations of personal financial advantage – and consequent political advantage. Without a change in political culture, Britain cannot change the dependency culture that has inadvertently been created.

It is time for a declaration of war: the 'War of Independence'. Its aim is to focus public attention on the benefits of bringing forward Britain's 'Independence Day'.

The aims of this war are not merely to increase economic growth and provide more families with jobs (although experience shows that it will do so). Nor are its aims to improve living standards and reduce social exclusion (although experience shows that these are the most likely outcomes). A War of Independence is just because dependence is bad and independence is good – good in itself. The overwhelming moral, political and economic arguments are in its favour. It is a necessary and just war.

The loss of individual independence is not a theoretical notion: it can be measured. Independence can be gauged by measuring the proportion of a citizen's working year that is spent earning money to pay to the government. It is possible to identify the day on which people stop working for the government and start working for themselves and their families. That day is Independence Day.

As little as forty years ago, soon after the establishment of the modern welfare state, and before privatization was even thought of, the government accounted for just thirty per cent of economic activity in Britain. In those days, Independence Day fell on 21 April.

In 2000, the tax burden reached £350 billion, equivalent to thirty-eight per cent of GDP. On this calculation, people worked for the government for all of the first five months of the year. So Independence Day in 2000 fell on 30 May. When the present government was elected three years ago Independence Day fell on 25 May. This year, it will be in June. The aim should be to move it back to 21 April, where it was in the 1950s, when tax was only thirty per cent of GDP.

Independence Day – the day on which people stop working for the government and start working for themselves and their families – should be declared a national holiday, a mark of progress towards the goal of greater independence for all. Independence Day should be a benchmark symbol, so that people will always be able to assess 'Are we going forwards or backwards?'

There would be three steps involved in such a reform of the present system: (1) a reduction of the role of government in transferring incomes between individuals; (2) exchanging the current mass of complex allowances for lower tax rates; and (3) integration of the government departments that deal with transfers.

These three changes, all detailed below, offer the scope to reduce the UK tax burden from over thirty-seven per cent of GDP to around thirty-three per cent – the first steps towards bringing forward Independence Day from 30 May to 21 April each year. They would invigorate the economy, restore work incentives to those on low incomes and improve the underlying pace of economic growth.

In addition to a dramatic increase in personal independence, these bold measures would release resources to finance an increase in spending on health and education.

1. A reduction in the role of government in transferring incomes between individuals

It goes against the grain that at present government gives with one hand and takes with another on the scale that it does. In 1948, payments that transferred money between individuals constituted just four per cent of national income. Today, as we have already seen, the figure is thirteen per cent.

A higher initial income tax threshold would render unnecessary a significant proportion of these transfer payments. This alone could deliver over half of the objective of the War of Independence.

The remaining two-fifths could be achieved in several ways, according to political preference. For example, in a number of areas there is scope for a transfer of economic decision-making from government to the individual, on the general principle that lower tax rates will enable individuals to relieve government of some of its present expenditures on their behalf: not a reduction in spending overall, just a reduction of *government* spending in favour of *individual* spending. The ultimate objective should be to diminish the role of government by a fifth – from thirty-eight per cent of the economy to thirty per cent – while enhancing the resources available for public health and education. The British people would then be able to celebrate their first victory in the War of Independence.

This fundamental reform of the tax and benefit system would enable cash payments from the government to be exchanged for protection from income tax payments to the government, thus reversing the trend of the past thirty years. A substantial restoration of the real value of the personal income tax threshold would be funded by the matched withdrawal of benefits currently paid to working households. Millions of benefit and pension supplements (or 'top-ups') would become redundant. In addition, occupational pensioners could elect to receive all or part of their state pension as a tax credit.

In the tax year 1998–9, there were 26.1 million individual taxpayers (the largest ever total). Back in 1958–9, there were only about twenty-one million. The main reason for this growth was that in the 1950s married couples with children received much larger tax allowances, lifting millions of them out of the tax system. The break-even point – defined as the level of earnings at which income tax paid is equal to the money received via tax allowances or child benefit – was equal to more than eighty per cent of average earnings (for all occupations) in 1960, compared with 47.7 per cent in 1997–8.

A radical reform of the tax and benefit system, so that the total income threshold for income tax and National Insurance payments was raised to about £15,000 per annum, would result in a loss of tax and National Insurance revenue of £30–40 billion under the present system. In principle, it should be possible to cancel out an equivalent amount of cash benefits and pensions without withdrawing support from individuals and families who are genuinely dependent. In the first instance, this reform would be strictly revenue-neutral, entailing parallel reductions in cash benefits and income tax receipts. However, in time, it should be expected to improve the efficiency of the economy and to raise the underlying rate of GDP growth.

Most working individuals with annual incomes below approximately £15,000 would simply cease to be taxpayers. Hardly anyone aged over sixty-five would pay income tax. Social security benefits would continue to be paid to able-bodied people out of work but seeking employment. For those working part-time or in low-paid jobs, the range of income over which social security benefits are phased out would no longer overlap with the threshold for payment of income tax. By separating the ranges of benefit withdrawal and income tax payment, the problem of very high marginal deduction rates would be greatly diminished. People would typically receive benefits or pensions, or pay income tax – but rarely both at the same time.

2. Exchanging the current mass of complex allowances for lower tax rates

Under the present system, the government has the capacity to levy gross tax charges on companies and individuals amounting to fifty-three per cent of GDP. Taxpayers are obliged to navigate a web of allowances, reliefs and exemptions in order to claim back sixteen per cent of national income, bringing the net tax take to thirty-eight per cent of GDP.

Apart from the expense and intrusion of such an arrangement, this system allows too much scope for 'hidden' tax increases, whereby the impact of increases is diluted by their being presented as alterations to allowances. An alternative, simplified system is needed, in which the web of allowances is simply exchanged for lower taxation by raising the starting threshold for income tax. The result would be a dramatically more transparent and open system, comprehensible to all.

3. Integration of the government departments that deal with transfers

A number of other advantages would flow from this radical rearrangement of the tax and benefit system. The administration of personal income tax by the Inland Revenue would be merged with the Department of Social Security and the Benefits and Contributions Agencies, allowing a comprehensive pooling of tax, contributions, benefits and pensions data. The recurring costs of administering the system would fall dramatically, due to the simplification of tax allowances and the elimination of duplicated tax assessments and benefit payments. The combined caseload of these offices could be reduced by twenty to thirty per cent, perhaps more.

The integration of tax, National Insurance, benefits and pensions records would also improve the detection of benefit fraud. A deliberate structural break in the administration of benefit payments would purge the long-standing abuses of the system. For example, by re-registering the National Insurance numbers of all adults, redundant numbers could be deleted from the system and any payments to them discontinued. This could yield far greater savings than costly and socially divisive snooping initiatives. A further reduction in the cost of fraudulent claims could be achieved by introducing 'smart' National Insurance cards to replace benefit order books, and electronic transfers to replace Giro cheques. Twenty-first century payment security technology is more than capable of rising to this challenge.

The annual savings from this reorganization and rationalization of the tax and benefit system, coupled with a sharp reduction in benefit fraud, could release £5 billion of extra funding for health and education. However, there would also be dynamic gains from such a thorough overhaul of the system. Not least, the higher starting threshold for income tax could be expected to restore earnings incentives and promote employment and GDP growth. *Table 7* provides an illustration of the possible impact of the three proposals outlined above.

In the last year, events have occurred that make it possible for the government to implement such a simplification plan. The Chancellor of the Exchequer has just collected the first instalment of a £22.5 billion bonanza resulting from the auction of third-generation mobile phone licences.

In addition, the UK (like the USA) is reaping massive, dual economic benefits. Buoyant financial markets have swelled the earnings and capital gains of a sizeable number of individuals, bringing significant additional income tax and capital gains tax revenues. Increases in stock-market turnover and levels have also increased government tax receipts from stamp duty. As a result, total tax receipts rose by six per cent last year, double the rate of GDP growth. At the same time, government expenditure on servicing debt has fallen dramatically as a result of historically low interest rates. The net result of these two factors is an unexpected £44 billion surplus in the public finances over the next four years.

What better use could there be for these gains than to smooth the transition to a permanently lower tax burden and a greatly

Table 7. Source of planned reductions in public expenditure and taxation

1997–8 values	Actual £ billion	Proposed £ billion	Difference £ billion	% of GDP
Reduction in public expenditure				
Proposal				
1. Savings from reduction in overlapping cash payments	105.2	70.2	−35.0	−4.3
2. Savings from integration of government departments and reduction in benefit fraud		5.0	−5.0	−0.6
Health and education funding	**71.5**	**76.5**	**+5.0**	**+0.6**
Total net reduction in public expenditure			−35.0	−4.3
Reduction in taxation				
Proposal				
1. Cost of raising initial personal income tax threshold			−55.0	−6.8
2. Reduction in income tax allowance			+20.0	+2.5
Total reduction in tax revenue			−35.0	−4.3

N.B. These changes are consistent with reducing the UK tax burden to 33 per cent of GDP.

simplified tax system, with all the long-term benefits that would bring to Britain's growth and competitiveness? What better investment could be made than one that returns income, independence and responsibility to its citizens? Within five years, the

UK could restore fairness, transparency and simplicity to the financial affairs of millions of households, and reduce the overall tax burden from thirty-eight to thirty-three per cent of GDP into the bargain.

Governments would be obliged to display greater transparency in their tax policies. Full disclosure would mean they could not hide from the political consequences of their tax actions. By exchanging the mass of complex allowances for lower tax rates, the huge gulf between the gross and net tax systems could be eliminated. The scope for 'stealth' taxes could be reduced. The hidden effects of fiscal drag could be neutralized. The system could be revitalized and restructured to reflect the New Enlightenment, for the benefit of all.

There are those who will say this cannot be done – there are no new ideas under the sun. But it can. For example, somebody once had the idea of giving council tenants the right to buy their own homes. That one concept alone turned dozens of marginal seats into safe Tory seats at the following election.

History shows that radical ideas tend to divide people. On one side are arranged those who say that nothing can be done, joined by those who think that nothing needs to be done. On the other side are aligned those people – as Disraeli once was – who believe something has to be done and that it can be done. This proposal is dedicated to the latter group.

As well as benefiting Britain, fighting and winning the War of Independence will improve the electoral prospects of the Conservative Party.

As Chapter Two showed, for many years there has been a direct correlation between voting intention and party ratings on 'tax' and 'managing the economy'. *Figure 7* illustrates how a government's reputation for economic management is particularly important when a general election is due. By 1997, the incoming Labour government was judged to have superior economic com-

Figure 7. The government and the economy
On balance do you agree or disagree that 'in the long term, this government's policies will improve the state of Britain's economy'? *Source: MORI British Public Opinion.*

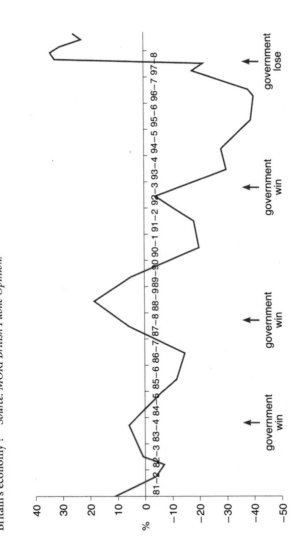

petence to that of the outgoing Conservative government.

The Conservative Party lost its economic credentials in autumn 1992 when sterling was ejected from the ERM. The depth of the recession in the early 1990s, while sterling was in the ERM and the government was unable to lower interest rates, made a large hole in the government's finances. This required the tax burden to be increased sharply soon after the economy emerged from recession, thus tarnishing the party's 'low tax' image (*Figure 8*). By 1997, New Labour was able to convince the British public that the economy was safe in their hands and that income tax rates would not be increased.

Until the 1997 election, 'low tax' had been an important part of the Conservative Party's presentation of its economic case to the electorate. This is ironic because income tax is a Tory invention. Income tax was first introduced by a Tory Prime Minister, Pitt the Younger. It was only abolished in 1816 by a revolt against Liverpool's Tory government by radicals and Whigs, led by the ultra-radical Henry Brougham who argued that income tax was 'an engine that should not be left at the disposal of extravagant ministers'.

Throughout the post-war period, Conservatives were considered the low tax party, Labour the high tax party. When the Conservatives won four elections in a row, in the 1970s, '80s and '90s, tax was a central issue. In exit polls, 'tax' was the number-one 'reason for not voting Labour' when Labour lost the 1992 election. Labour's pollster Philip Gould testifies to the power of taxation in the Conservative armoury when he writes of that election,

On 12 December, I delivered the 1992 'War Book': the complete campaign for the election. I said our first weakness was tax, our second, lack of trust. The Tories' core message would be 'You can't trust Labour'. Their key attacks would be on tax ... and the core themes would be Kinnock against Major and

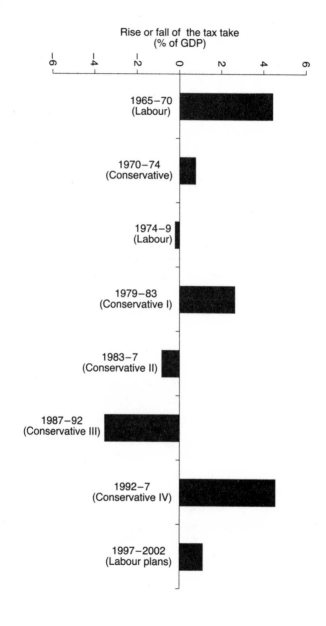

Figure 8. Political analysis of changes in overall taxation
Sources: Inland Revenue Statistics and the Pre-Budget Report, November 1998.

high tax Labour against low tax Conservatives. Less than four weeks after I wrote the War Book the Conservatives hit us on tax, with the 'Tax Bombshell' campaign on 6 January 1992. I was out of the country and heard the news over the telephone. As the news went on and on – National Insurance, top rate of tax, £1000 per family – I knew we were finished. And less than three months later the Tories launched their election campaign, with the slogan 'You Can't Trust Labour'.

Today, 'tax' is one of the few issues where the Conservatives' poll ratings are ahead of Labour's – a folk-memory of other days. But, as seen in Chapter Two, some in the Conservative Party turned away from tax as a political issue when New Labour leaders woke up and adopted a 'low tax' approach. Instead of wishing to rebuild Conservative strength on tax, they planned to drop it off the Tory agenda because it was a reminder of the 'money-obsessed' image they associated with past Tory failure.

It is time to put it back on. But in a manner that reflects the sophistication and wariness of the modern British electorate. An informed debate about the wider role of taxation and government spending will help the Conservative Party to win electoral respect and success. Radical proposals can excite the imagination. But the worst of all worlds would be a continuation of the status quo – for the electorate has grown weary of some politicians' glib or pat answers to the long-standing and intractable problems of tax and spending on public services. Their answers are unsuited to the New Enlightenment.

Orson Welles once memorably told this story:

Now I am going to tell you about a scorpion. This scorpion wanted to cross a river, so he asked the frog to carry him. 'No,' said the frog. 'No, thank you. If I let you on my back, you may sting me, and the sting of the scorpion is death.' 'Now, where,' asked the scorpion, 'is the logic of that?' (For scorpions always try to be logical.) 'If I sting you, you will die and I will drown.' So the frog was convinced and allowed the scorpion on his back. But just in the middle of the river he felt a terrible pain and realized that, after all, the scorpion had stung him. 'Logic!' cried the dying frog as he started under, bearing the scorpion down with him. 'There is no logic in this!' 'I know,' said the scorpion, 'but I can't help it – it's my character.'

Welles concluded the tale with a toast: 'Let's drink to character.'

The moral of the story is a simple one: the essential need of people to understand their own nature. Welles' advice, like Shakespeare's in *Hamlet*, was 'To thine own self be true'. This conforms with the wisdom of the ancients. The injunction of the oracle at Delphi was 'Know Thyself'. Those who failed to heed its warning met a sorry end: Oedipus, being ignorant of who he really was, went on to murder his father and marry his mother. Bertrand Russell also advised that a clear sense of identity, founded in self-knowledge, is 'the only possible protection against the disappointments and disillusionments to which the self-deceiver is liable'.

The historic identity of Conservatism, in the two centuries from Burke to Thatcher, is a belief in self-determination, inner-directedness, individuality, autonomy. In the New Enlightenment of the twenty-first century those qualities of independence will be the most prized of the virtues. By pursuing independence the Conservative Party will be true to its character: the true interpreter of the New Enlightenment, and its chief beneficiary.

In the new century, when all voters will be as clever as Harvard Business School graduates, they are already looking ahead. And they don't like what they see. They have real economic concerns: 'How will I protect my parents' old age?' 'How will my children's university fees be paid?' 'Who will pay for my family's medical care?' 'How do I pay the mortgage when my tax is always going up?' 'Will there be a proper pension left for me?' The answers to those questions will prove the acid test of Conservative thinking in the New Enlightenment.

To answer them, Conservatives will have to seize the helm of Professor Oakeshott's boat, study the compass bearings, and set course for Independence. For the Conservative Party in the twenty-first century there should be no shame in an aim, no ban on a plan.

On the contrary, a clear sense of purpose, a certain idealism, a marching-tune people can respond to are – as they once were for Disraeli – the essential preconditions for Conservative security and happiness, the way to make this the next Conservative century.

Appendix 1

Independence Day

Independence Day expresses the overall tax burden in terms of days per year. It calculates how much of the year the average income earner spends in financing the government's budget. When Independence Day is reached, individuals have fulfilled their obligations to the government and for the remainder of the year they enjoy full discretion over their earnings.

Independence Day represents the total tax revenue, including indirect taxes, local taxes and National Insurance contributions, paid annually by a taxpayer with average income, as a percentage of total income. For practical purposes, it is calculated as general government tax revenue in relation to the net national product (NNP). NNP differs from the more familiar GDP in two ways. First, NNP adds in the net property and entrepreneurial income of UK citizens from abroad (which totalled £15 billion in 1998). Second, NNP subtracts capital consumption (i.e. depreciation of fixed capital assets), which amounted to £88 billion in 1998. NNP is therefore smaller than GDP, making the ratio of tax revenue to NNP slightly larger than in relation to GDP. For 1998, the ratio of tax to NNP was 41.1 per cent as compared with the 37.1 per cent of GDP reported in the March 2000 Budget Report.

The rationale for using a net rather than a gross measure of national income is straightforward. Since depreciation is an expense – expenditure that must be set aside in order to replace worn-out fixed assets if the economy is to function properly – it should be deducted when calculating the tax burden. The only difference between depreciation and other, mainly corporate, expenditures is that it is not an immediate drain on corporate cash flow. An invoice for depreciation does not arrive each 31 December, but whenever companies replace fixed assets they are implicitly drawing on their cash reserves, and this is represented by the annual depreciation charge.

The use of multi-year budget changes and the replacement of family credit (which was recorded as benefit expenditure) by the working families tax credit (which is recorded as a negative tax) have muddied the waters in terms of comparability of the tax burden from year to year. Last year, the Adam Smith Institute decided to average out the changes over the 1997–9 period in order to create a clearer comparison with previous years. The average tax burden for 1997–9 equated to 151 days, as against 146 days in 1996. The use of so-called 'stealth' taxes, tax changes made other than at budget time or preannounced changes that have an impact in distant years, has continued in the 2000 budget. The preannounced abolition of the married couple's allowance and mortgage interest relief took effect in April 2000, but the children's tax credit which replaces the married couple's allowance will not be introduced for another year.

After adding back in the effect of the working families tax credit, the tax burden is projected to rise from 37.1 per cent in 1999–2000 (on the Treasury's own calculations) to 37.5 per cent in 2000–2001 and 38 per cent in 2001–2. The stage is set for Independence Day to slip into the beginning of June even if the UK economy performs well.

Appendix 2

Schedule of benefits

Attendance allowance

higher rate
lower rate

Child benefit

only, elder or eldest for whom child benefit is payable (couple)
only, elder or eldest for whom child benefit is payable (lone parent)
each subsequent child

Child's special allowance

see note on child dependency increase

Council tax benefit

personal allowances
   single
   18 to 24
   25 or over
   lone parent – 18 or over
   couple – one or both over 18
dependent children
   birth to September following eleventh birthday
   from September following eleventh birthday to September following
      sixteenth birthday
   from September following sixteenth birthday to day before nineteenth
      birthday
premiums
   family
   family (lone parent rate)

pensioner
  single
  couple
pensioner (enhanced)
  single
  couple
pensioner (higher)
  single
  couple
disability
severe disability
  single
  couple (one qualifies)
  couple (both qualify)
disabled child
carer
allowance for personal expenses for claimants in hospital
  higher rate
  lower rate
non-dependant deductions
  aged 18 or over and in remunerative work
    gross income less than £118
    gross income: £118–203.99
    gross income: £204–254.99
    gross income: £255 or more
  others aged 18 or over
alternative maximum council tax benefit – second adult on income
  support or income-based jobseeker's allowance
  second adult's gross income under £118
  second adult's gross income £118–154.99
capital
  upper limit
  amount disregarded
  child's limit
  upper limit for permanent resident of residential care/nursing home
  amount disregarded for permanent resident of residential care/nursing home
  tariff income – £1 for every complete £250 or part thereof between

amount of capital disregarded and capital upper limit
earnings disregards
    where disability premium awarded
    various specified employments
    lone parent
    where the claimant has a partner
    single claimant
    where carer premium awarded
    childcare charges
    childcare charges (two or more children)
    other income disregards
    maintenance disregard
    war disablement pension and war widow's pension
    certain voluntary and charitable payments
    student loan
    student's covenanted income
    income from boarders – disregard the fixed amount (£20) plus 50 per cent of the balance of the charge
    30 hours adult allowance in disability working allowance
    30 hours adult credit in family credit
    expenses for subtenants
        furnished or unfurnished
        where heating is included, additional

Dependency increases

adult dependency increases
    for spouse or person looking after children
    with retirement pension on own insurance
    long-term incapacity benefit
    unemployability supplement
    severe disablement allowance
    invalid care allowance
    short-term incapacity benefit if beneficiary over pension age
    maternity allowance/short-term incapacity benefit
child dependency increases
    with retirement pension, widow's benefit, short-term incapacity benefit at the higher rate, long-term incapacity benefit, invalid care allowance, severe disablement allowance, higher rate industrial

death benefit, unemployability supplement, and short-term incapacity benefit if beneficiary over pension age

Disability living allowance

care component
   highest
   middle
   lowest
mobility component
   higher
   lower

Disability working allowance

adult allowance
single people
couples/lone parents
30 hours allowance
child allowance
   from birth
   from September following eleventh birthday
   from September following sixteenth birthday
applicable amount (i.e. taper threshold)
   single people
   couples/lone parents
   disabled child's allowance
capital
   upper limit
   amount disregarded
   child's limit
   tariff income – £1 for every complete £250 or part thereof between amount of capital disregarded and capital upper limit
disregards
   maintenance disregard
   war disablement pension and war widow's pension
   certain voluntary and charitable payments
   student loan
   student's covenanted income

income from boarders – disregard the fixed amount (£20) plus 50 per
    cent of the balance of the charge
childcare charges
childcare charges (two or more children)
expenses for subtenants
    furnished or unfurnished
    where heating is included, additional

Earnings rules

invalid care allowance
limit of earnings from councillor's allowance
therapeutic earnings limit
industrial injuries unemployability
supplement permitted earnings level (annual amount)
war pensioner's unemployability supplement permitted earnings level
(annual amount)
adult dependency increases with short-term incapacity benefit where
    claimant is
    (a) under pension age
    (b) over pension age
maternity allowance
retirement pension, long-term incapacity benefit, severe disablement
    allowance, unemployability supplement where dependant
    (a) is living with claimant
    (b) still qualifies for the tapered earnings rule
severe disablement allowance where dependant not living with claimant
invalid care allowance
child dependency increases – levels at which child dependency increases
    are affected by earnings of claimant's spouse or partner
    for first child
    for each subsequent child

Family credit

adult credit
30 hours credit
child credits
    from birth

from September following eleventh birthday
from September following sixteenth birthday
applicable amount (i.e. threshold)
capital
    upper limit
    amount disregarded
    child's limit
    assumed income from capital – £1 for every £250 or part of £250
        between amount of capital disregarded and capital upper limit
disregards
    maintenance disregard
    war disablement pension and war widow's pension
    certain voluntary and charitable payments
    student loan
    student's covenanted income
    income from boarders – disregard the fixed amount (£20) plus 50 per
        cent of the balance of the charge
    childcare charges
    childcare charges (two or more children)
    expenses for subtenants
        furnished or unfurnished
        where heating is included, additional

Guardian's allowance

See note on child dependency increase

Hospital downrating

20 per cent rate
40 per cent rate

Housing benefit

personal allowances
    single
        16 to 24
        25 or over
    lone parent
        under 18

      18 or over

    couple

      both under 18

      one or both over 18

    dependent children

      birth to September following eleventh birthday

      from September following eleventh birthday to September following sixteenth birthday

      from September following sixteenth birthday to day before nineteenth birthday

premiums

    family

    family (lone parent rate)

    pensioner

      single

      couple

    pensioner (enhanced)

      single

      couple

    pensioner (higher)

      single

      couple

    disability

      single

      couple

    severe disability

      single

      couple (one qualifies)

      couple (both qualify)

    disabled child

    carer

    allowance for personal expenses for claimants in hospital

      higher rate

      lower rate

    non-dependant deductions, rent rebates and allowances aged 25 and over, in receipt of income support or income-based job seeker's allowance aged 18 or over, not in remunerative work or gross income less than £80

aged 18 or over and in remunerative work
   gross income less than £80
   gross income £80–117.99
   gross income £118–154.99
   gross income £155–203.99
   gross income £204–254.99
   gross income £255 and above
service charges for fuel
   heating
   hot water
   lighting
   cooking
amount ineligible for meals
   three or more meals per day
      single claimant
      each person in family aged 16 or over
      each child under 16
   less than three meals per day
      single claimant
      each person in family aged 16 or over
      each child under 16
   breakfast only – claimant and each member of family
capital
   upper limit
   amount disregarded
   child's limit
   upper limit for permanent resident of residential care/nursing home
   amount disregarded for permanent resident of residential care/nursing home
   tariff income – £1 for every complete £250 or part thereof between amount of capital disregarded and capital upper limit
earnings disregards
   where disability premium awarded
   various specified employments
   lone parent
   where the claimant has a partner
   single claimant
   where carer premium awarded

childcare charges
childcare charges (two or more children)
other income disregards
  maintenance disregards
  war disablement pension and war widow's pension
  certain voluntary and charitable payments
  student loan
  student's covenanted income
  income from boarders – disregard the fixed amount (£20) plus 50 per
    cent of the balance of the charge
  30 hour adult allowance in disability working allowance
  30 hour adult credit in family credit
  expenses for subtenants
    furnished or unfurnished
    where heating is included, additional

Incapacity benefit

long-term incapacity benefit
short-term incapacity benefit (under pension age)
  lower rate
  higher rate
short-term incapacity benefit (over pension age)
  lower rate
  higher rate
increase of long-term incapacity benefit for age
  higher rate
  lower rate
invalidity allowance (transitional)
  higher rate
  middle rate
  lower rate

Income support

personal allowances
  single
    under 18 – usual rate
    under 18 – higher rate payable

        in specific circumstances
        18 to 24
        25 or over
    lone parent
        under 18 – usual rate
        under 18 – higher rate payable
        in specific circumstances
        18 or over
    couple
        both under 18
        one or both 18 or over
        dependent children
            birth to September following eleventh birthday
            from September following eleventh birthday to September fol-
                lowing sixteenth birthday
            from September following sixteenth birthday to day before
                nineteenth birthday
residential allowance except Greater London
    Greater London
premiums
    family
    family (lone parent rate)
    pensioner
        single
        couple
    pensioner (enhanced)
        single
        couple
    pensioner (higher)
        single
        couple
    disability
        single
        couple
    severe disability
        single
        couple (one qualifies)
        couple (both qualify)

disabled child

carer

maximum amounts for accommodation and meals in residential care
homes

old age

very dependent elderly

mental disorder (not handicap)

drug/alcohol dependence

mental handicap

physical disablement

(a) (under pension age)

(b) (over pension age)

others

maximum Greater London increase

nursing homes

mental disorder (not handicap)

drug/alcohol dependence

mental handicap

terminal illness

physical disablement

(a) (under pension age)

(b) (over pension age)

others (including elderly)

maximum Greater London increase

amounts for meals where these cannot be purchased with the
accommodation

(daily rate)

breakfast

midday meal

evening meal

allowances for personal expenses for claimants in private and voluntary
residential care and nursing homes

personal expenses

dependent children

(a) under 11

(b) 11 to 15

(c) 16 to 17

(d) age 18

capital
    upper limit
    amount disregarded
    child's limit
    upper limit for permanent residents of residential care/nursing homes
    amount disregarded for permanent residents of residential care/nursing homes
    tariff income – £1 for every complete £250 or part thereof between amount of capital disregarded and capital upper limit
disregards
    standard earnings
    couple's earnings
    higher earnings
    war disablement pension and war widow's pension
    voluntary and charitable payments
    student loan
    student's covenanted income
    income from boarders – disregard the fixed amount (£20) plus 50 per cent of the balance of the charge
    expenses for subtenants
        furnished or unfurnished
        where heating is included, additional

Industrial death benefit

widow's pension
    higher rate
    lower rate

Industrial disablement pension

18 and over, or under 18 with dependants
    100 per cent; 90 per cent; 80 per cent; 70 per cent; 60 per cent; 50 per cent; 40 per cent; 30 per cent; 20 per cent
under 18
    100 per cent; 90 per cent; 80 per cent; 70 per cent; 60 per cent; 50 per cent; 40 per cent; 30 per cent; 20 per cent
maximum life gratuity (lump sum)
unemployability supplement plus where appropriate an increase for early

incapacity
    higher rate
    middle rate
    lower rate
maximum reduced earnings allowance
maximum retirement allowance
constant attendance allowance
    exceptional rate
    intermediate rate
    normal maximum rate
    part-time rate
exceptionally severe disablement allowance

Jobseeker's allowance

contribution-based jobseeker's allowance – personal rates
    under 18
    18 to 24
    25 or over
income-based jobseeker's allowance – personal allowances
    under 18
    18 to 24
    25 or over
    lone parent
        under 18 – usual rate
        under 18 – higher rate payable
        in specific circumstances
        18 or over
    couple
        both under 18
        both under 18, one disabled
        both under 18, with responsibility for a child
        one under 18, one 18–24
        one under 18, one 25 or over
        both 18 or over
    dependent children
        birth to September following eleventh birthday
        from September following eleventh birthday to September
        following sixteenth birthday

mental handicap
terminal illness
physical disablement
　　(under pension age)
others (including elderly)
maximum Greater London increase
amounts for meals where these cannot be purchased within the
accommodation
(daily rate)
breakfast
midday meal
evening meal
allowances for personal expenses for claimants in private and voluntary
residential care and nursing homes
personal expenses
dependent children
　　under 11
　　11 to 15
　　16 to 17
　　age 18
hospital
higher rate
lower rate
local authority (Pt lll) accommodation
of which, personal expenses
housing costs
deduction for non-dependants
　　aged 25 and over, in receipt of income support or income-based
　　　job seeker's allowance
　　aged 18 or over, not in remunerative work or
　　gross income less than £80
　　gross income £80–117.99
　　gross income £118–154.99
　　gross income £155–203.99
　　gross income £204–254.99
　　gross income £255 and above
for direct payments
deductions from jobseeker's allowance (incapacity benefit)

cent of the balance of the charge
expenses for subtenants
    furnished or unfurnished
    where heating is included, additional

Maternity allowance

lower rate
higher rate

Pneumoconiosis, byssinosis, workmen's compensation (supplementation) and other schemes

incapacity allowance (maximum)
partial disablement allowance
unemployability supplement, plus where appropriate increases for early
    incapacity
    higher rate
    middle rate
    lower rate
constant attendance allowance
    exceptional rate
    intermediate rate
    normal maximum rate
    part-time rate
exceptionally severe disablement allowance
lesser incapacity allowance
    maximum rate of allowance
    based on loss of earnings

Retirement pension

category A or B
category B (lower) – husband's insurance
category C or D – non-contributory
category C (lower) – non-contributory
additional pension
increments to
    basic and additional pensions
    contracted-out deductions (pre-April 1988 earnings)

graduated retirement benefit
contracted-out deductions (April 1988 – April 1996 earnings)
(3.0 per cent paid by schemes)
graduated retirement benefit (unit)
graduated retirement benefit (inherited)
additional at age 80

Severe disablement allowance

basic rate
age-related addition (from December 1990)
higher rate
middle rate
lower rate

Statutory maternity pay

earnings threshold
lower rate

Statutory sick pay

earnings threshold
standard rate

War pensions

disablement pension (100 per cent rates)
   officer
   other ranks
age allowances
   40–50 per cent
   over 50 per cent but not over 70 per cent
   over 70 per cent but not over 90 per cent
   over 90 per cent
disablement gratuity
   specified minor injury (minimum)
   specified minor injury (maximum)
   unspecified minor injury (minimum)
   unspecified minor injury (maximum)

unemployability allowance
    personal
    adult dependency increase
    increase for first child
    increase for subsequent children
invalidity allowance
    higher rate
    middle rate
    lower rate
constant attendance allowance
    exceptional rate
    intermediate rate
    normal maximum rate
    part-time rate
comforts allowance
    higher rate
    lower rate
mobility supplement
allowance for lowered standard of occupation
exceptionally severe disablement allowance
severe disablement occupational allowance
clothing allowance
education allowance
war widow's pension
    widow (private)
    widow (NCO)
    widow (officer)
    childless widow under 40 (private)
    childless widow under 40 (NCO)
    childless widow under 40 (officer)
supplementary pension
age allowance
    age 65 to 69
    age 70 to 79
    age 80 and over
children's allowance
    increase for first child
        (adjusted for child benefit increase)

increase for subsequent children
orphan's pension
   increase for first child
     (adjusted for child benefit increase)
   increase for subsequent children
unmarried dependant living as spouse
rent allowance
adult orphan's pension
widower's pension
   private
   officer

Widow's benefit

widow's payment (lump sum)
widowed mother's allowance
widow's pension
   standard rate
   age-related: age 54 (49); 53 (48); 52 (47); 51 (46); 50 (45); 49 (44); 48
     (43); 47 (42); 46 (41); 45 (40) (for deaths occurring before 11 April
     1988 refer to age-points shown in brackets)

scheme A

credit
   couple
   single 25 and over
   single under 25
   for working over 30 hours per week
applicable amount (i.e. taper threshold)
   couple
   single 25 and over
   single under 25

scheme B

credit
   couple
   single 25 and over
   single under 25
   for working over 30 hours per week

applicable amount (i.e. taper threshold)
    couple
    single 25 and over
    single under 25

both schemes
capital upper limit
    amount disregarded
    tariff income – £1 for every complete £250 or part thereof between
        amount of capital disregarded and capital upper limit

Appendix 3

Schedule of tax allowances, reliefs and exemptions

Tax allowances

occupational pension schemes

contributions to personal pensions (including retirement annuity premiums and FSAVCs)

life assurance premiums (for contracts made prior to 14 March 1984)

private medical insurance premiums for the over-60s

mortgage interest

approved profit sharing schemes

approved discretionary share option schemes

approved savings-related share option schemes

venture capital trusts

enterprise investment scheme

profit-related pay

first £30,000 of payments on termination of employment

interest on National Savings certificates including index-linked certificates

Premium Bond prizes

SAYE

income of charities

foreign service allowance paid to crown servants abroad

first £8000 of reimbursed relocation packages provided by employers

gains arising on disposal of only or main residence

retirement relief

reinvestment relief

agricultural property relief

business property relief

heritage property and maintenance funds

transfers to charities on death

double taxation relief

reduced rate of corporation tax on policyholders' fraction of profits contracted-out rebate occupational schemes, of which

    occupational schemes deducted from National Insurance contributions received

    occupational schemes (COMPS) paid by Contributions Agency direct to scheme

    personal pensions

married couple's allowance

age-related allowances

additional personal allowance for one-parent family

relief for maintenance payments

child special allowance

guardian's allowance

National Insurance child dependency additions

severe disablement allowance

allowances to rehabilitees

maternity allowance

£10 Christmas bonus for pensioners

pensions and annuities paid to holders of the Victoria Cross and certain other gallantry awards

children's allowance to forces' widows

disability working allowance

widow's payments

benefit of medical expenses paid by employer when employee falls sick when abroad

benefit of alterations to accommodation by reason of employment

special security measures

certain expenses of MPs

benefit of workplace sports facilities

outplacement counselling for redundant employees

accelerated capital allowances for Enterprise Zones

Tax exemptions

British government securities where owner not ordinarily resident in the United Kingdom

child benefit (including one-parent benefit)

long-term incapacity benefit

industrial disablement benefits

attendance allowance

disability living allowance

war disablement benefits

war widow's pension

small companies' reduced rate of corporation tax

indexation allowance and rebasing to March 1982

taper relief

annual exempt amount (half of the individual's exemption for trustees)

gains accrued but unrealized at death

nil rate inheritance tax band for chargeable transfers not exceeding the
    threshold

inheritance tax on transfers on death to surviving spouses

stamp duty on transfers of land and property where the consideration
    does not exceed the threshold

reduced National Insurance contributions for self-employed not attrib-
    utable to reduce benefit eligibility

widow's bereavement allowance

blind person's allowance

first £70 of National Savings Bank ordinary account interest

short-term lower rate incapacity benefit

certain personal incidental expenses

charitable donations under the payroll giving scheme

student maintenance awards

trade unions' investment income applied to provident benefits

agricultural societies' profits on shows

officials and agents of overseas governments, etc.

visiting forces, other than UK citizens

intergovernmental organizations

unremitted income of taxpayers resident but not domiciled in the UK

certain statutory and public bodies and local authorities

funds held for reducing the National Debt

income of Trustee Savings Banks from investments with the National
    Debt commissioners

discount element of certain gilts issued at a discount

accrued income of small investors whose nominal value of holding of
    securities does not exceed £5000

subsidized canteen meals provided for an employer's staff generally

benefit of living accommodation and associated costs provided to certain
    groups of employees

beneficial loans below £5000

benefit of entertainment provided for employees by third parties

car parking at or near an employee's place of work

retraining expenditure

friendly societies

futures and options – examples for authorized unit trusts and pension
schemes

workplace nurseries

unit trusts from full rate of corporation tax (reduced rate applies)

company car accessories for the disabled

unremitted gains of taxpayers resident but not domiciled in the UK

gains of charities and scientific research organizations

gains of approved pension schemes

gains of unit trusts for exempt unitholders

gains accruing to authorized unit trusts and approved investment trusts

actual and deemed gains of settlements on death of life tenant

gains arising on disposal of

motor cars

chattels which are wasting assets

other chattels if value is £6000 or less on disposal

assets by way of gifts to the nation

savings certificates and securities issued under the National Loans Act
1968

decorations for valour

contracts for deferred annuities

interests under a settlement

currency for personal expenditure outside the UK

life assurance policies

gains arising from

betting winnings

compensation or damages for wrong or injury

grants of purchased annuities

lifetime transfers between spouses

gifts of £3000 each year

gifts of £250 per donee

normal gifts out of income

gifts in consideration of marriage

lifetime transfers to charities

gifts to political parties

foreign pensions and foreign armed forces pay

cash options under approved annuity schemes

certain savings by persons domiciled in the Channel Islands or the Isle of
   Man

foreign currency bank accounts

waivers of dividends and remuneration

reversionary interests

transfers to employee trusts

settled property passing to settlor, spouse or widow

accumulation and maintenance settlements

trusts for mentally or physically disabled

death on active service

trade or professional compensation funds

charitable trusts

employee and newspaper trusts

protective trusts

superannuation schemes

distributions out of discretionary trusts to charities, political parties, etc.

estate duty surviving spouse settlements

transfers of land to registered housing associations

transfers of stock on sale to market makers or recognized intermediaries

transfers between associated companies

transfers of building society shares

issues or transfers of bearer instruments in foreign currencies

transfers of Commonwealth government stocks and certain loan stocks

transfers to a minister of the crown

transfers to charities

other minor stamp duty exemptions

transfers under stock borrowing and sale and repurchase arrangements

limitation of duty payable on purchases of public sector dwellings

limitation of duty payable on borrowings of stock by market makers

purchases by issuing houses in connection with public issues

purchases by market makers or recognized intermediaries

purchases under stock borrowing and sale and repurchase arrangements

purchases of securities by broker/dealers where the securities are resold
   within seven days

purchases by managers of units under a unit trust scheme

purchases by charities
purchases of certain bearer instruments

Tax relief for

instalment relief on share options exercised outside approved schemes
expenditure on property managed as one estate
farming, etc., averaging of profits
post-trading expenditure
rent-a-room
special security measures
professional subscriptions
vocational training
relief to investment companies for losses on unquoted shares in trading
    companies
relief for trading losses against capital gains
quick succession relief
taper relief on transfers between three and seven years before death
double taxation relief
woodlands relief

Rollover/holdover relief for

gifts of assets
transfers of businesses to companies
transfers of non-United Kingdom trades to non-resident companies
sales of shares to employee share ownership trusts
replacement of business assets
compensation used to restore damaged assets
small part-disposals of land
small capital distributions in respect of shares
reorganizations of share capital
reconstructions and amalgamations of companies
gains on disposals
    within a group of companies
    of shares in return for gilts on compulsory acquisition
    assets between spouses
    other qualifying reliefs

exit charge on company migration

Allowances and reliefs for

pre-trading expenditure
demergers
industrial and provident societies
co-operative associations
housing associations
company's purchase of its own shares
qualifying interest on loans not for the purchase of owner-occupied, etc.,
    property
schedule E work expenses
foreign earnings of employees working abroad for 365 days or more: one
    hundred per cent deduction
certain income of non-residents received through UK representatives
foreign pensions
Lloyd's underwriters: special reserve fund arrangement
interest paid by companies on quoted Eurobonds
income tax relief for losses on unquoted shares in trading companies
certain foreign travel expenses
transfers of securities under approved stock lending arrangements
payments to trustees for approved profit sharing schemes
payments to relevant scientific research associations
payments for technical education relevant to a taxpayer's trade
business contributions to Training and Enterprise Councils and Local
    Enterprise Councils
employee priority allocations in public share offers
payments to ESOP trusts
employer-provided work-related training
payments from sickness and unemployment insurance policies
indexation allowance and rebasing to March 1982 for companies
double taxation of capital gains realized by individuals or trustees
losses on disposals of assets between spouses
chattels exceeding £6000 in value (marginal relief)
disposals by political party associations following boundary changes
loans to traders
gains on stock lending
irrecoverable bonds

129

land acquired by authorities with compulsory purchase powers
falls in value of property before death or after death
interest-free instalments
double charges
Lloyd's premiums trust funds
gifts for the maintenance of the family
gifts for national purposes or for public benefit
government securities owned by non-United Kingdom domiciled
    persons

Appendix 4

Budget 1999 measures to alter allowances, reliefs and exemptions

Companies

corporation tax: new ten per cent rate for the smallest companies from April 2000

extension of first year capital allowances for SMEs at forty per cent, for one year

research and development tax credit

tax relief for employer-loaned computers

individual learning accounts: making employer contributions to employee ILAs tax and NICs free

abolition of vocational training relief (VTR)

Income tax

indexation of most allowances and limits

new ten per cent rate from April 1999

basic rate reduced to twenty-two per cent from April 2000

National Insurance contributions

indexation of thresholds

alignment of threshold with income tax personal allowance, in two stages, beginning April 2000

increases to upper earnings limits for employee contributions in April 2000 and April 2001

reform of self-employment contribution rates and profits limits from April 2000

reduction in employer contribution rate by 0.5 percentage points from April 2001

Benefits

New Deal package for the over-50s: employment credit

income support: two week extension for lone parents moving into work

abolition of married couple's allowance from April 2000 for those born
after 5 April 1935

introduction of children's tax credit from April 2001
with increases in income support child premiums
and with increases in working families tax credit and disabled person's
tax credit

child benefit: indexation of rates and uprating from April 2000 to £15 per
week for first child and £10 per week for subsequent children

Sure Start maternity grant

maternity pay reforms

increasing personal allowances for older people

increased minimum income guarantee for pensioners

£100 winter allowance from 1999

abolition of mortgage interest relief from April 2000

countering avoidance in the provision of personal services

extension of employer National Insurance contributions to all benefits in
kind which are subject to income tax from April 2000

controlled foreign companies (CFCs): taxation of dividends

capital gains on sale of companies

stamp duty: compliance

VAT
changes to partial exemption rules
group treatment
enlarging of VAT exemption on financing arrangements
bringing supplies by certain organizations in line with trade unions
and professional bodies

taxation of reverse premiums

climate change levy

energy efficiency measures and support for renewable energy sources

green transport plans

increase in minor oils duties

hydrocarbon oil duty escalator

cut in duty on higher octane unleaded petrol

company car taxation: reduction in business mileage discounts from
April

landfill tax: introduction of five-year escalator

Vehicle excise duty (VED)

graduated VED – reduction of charge for small cars and indexation for others

new VED for heavy lorries

freeze on other lorry VED

Other

tobacco – aligning escalator with budget day, freeze on hand-rolled tobacco

alcohol – aligning revalorization point with budget day and freeze

gifts of equipment by businesses to charities

inheritance tax: index threshold

capital gains tax: rate adjustment

VAT: indexation of registration and deregistration thresholds

football clubs: assistance for transition to new accounting rules

revised rate of pools betting duty from 26.5 per cent to 17.5 per cent

removing the income tax charge on mobile phones

stamp duty: 2.5 per cent rate for transfer of land and property above £250,000 and 3.5 per cent above £500,000

increase in the rate of insurance premium tax by one percentage point (to five per cent)

VAT: option to tax land and property rules

Lloyd's insurance market: simplifying capital gains

Source: Financial Statement and Budget Report (HC 298, 1998–99)

Appendix 5

The administration of the new tax credits on employers

In December 1999, the Inland Revenue issued a twenty-page document entitled *An Employers' Guide to Tax Credits – Working Families Tax Credit (WFTC) and Disabled Person's Tax Credit (DPTC)* in order to prepare employers for the introduction of the new system from April 2000.

In its introduction, the document explains: 'The tax credits are worth more than the old benefits and aim to tackle both the unemployment trap and the poverty trap, which can sometimes put people off getting a job or increasing the number of hours they work.' The following extracts from the document give some idea of the complications, extra work and expense that its implementation involves:

> If you have a manual payroll … In order to pay tax credits to an employee you will have to use some or all of the PAYE tax, NICs and student loan deductions that you have deducted from your employees' pay. You therefore need to make sure that you have cash flow checks which will tell you in good time if you will not have enough money on hand to pay tax credits. If your tax credit payments are more than the deductions you make, you may apply to us for advance funding.

The reader is then referred to Section 6 of the document which helpfully addresses the following questions:

> In what circumstances can I ask for Inland Revenue funding?
> How do I apply?
> How soon do I apply for funding?
> How far in advance can I apply?

What information will I have to provide in order to get advance
   funding?
How will I know that my funding application has been accepted?
Will I receive all the funding I have applied for at once?
What if the Inland Revenue disagrees with my calculations?
How can I appeal?
How much notice do I have to give if I want funding?
What happens if I have met these conditions but the funding has just
   not arrived?
What happens if I find that I am going to be short of funds on pay-
   day?
Can I apply for funding even if I don't have a bank account?
Can I reduce or increase my initial funding application?
What happens if I no longer need funding?
How will my payroll system have to change?

Employers will have to be able to:

calculate the tax credits for the period from a daily rate;
pay the tax credit through the payroll;
enter this amount on the employee's payslip;
record the total tax credits paid in a tax year;
enter the total tax credits in the year for the employee on the P14 and
   P60;
enter the total tax credits for all employees in the year on the P35,
   together with the total amount of Inland Revenue funding for
   that year; and
complete certificates of payments when they stop paying tax credit
   earlier than the end of the period of responsibility.

These procedures apply to all employers from the smallest of small businesses to multinational corporations.

Bibliography

Ball, Stuart, *The Conservative Party Since 1945* (1998).

Berlin, Isaiah, *Four Essays on Liberty* (1979 edn).

Bhattacharyya, Dilip K., *The Hidden Economy: Estimates and Their Implications for Government Expenditure*, Deloitte & Touche Informal Economy Research Centre Working Paper No. 1 (November 1998).

Blake, Robert, *The Conservative Party from Peel to Churchill* (1970).

Burgess, Ronald, *Public Revenue Without Taxation* (1993 edn).

Butler, David, and Dennis Kavanagh, *The British General Election of 1997* (1997 edn).

Butler, Lord, *The Conservatives* (1977).

Bryant, A., *The Spirit of Conservatism* (1929).

Caragata, Patrick, *Why Are Your Taxes So High?* (February 1998).

Cattell, Raymond, *The Scientific Analysis of Personality* (1965 edn).

Centre for Policy Studies, *After the Landslide* (David Willetts MP with Richard Forsdyke) (September 1999).

Centre for Policy Studies, *Conservatism, Democracy and National Identity* (John O'Sullivan) (February 1999).

Chennels, Lucy, and Andrew Dilnot (eds.), *The IFS Green Budget* (London: Institute for Fiscal Studies, January 1999).

Churchill, Winston, *The People's Rights* (1970 edn).

Congdon, Tim, 'EMU and Tax Harmonization: How Much Will We Have to Pay?', Politeia lecture (26 January 1999).

Cowling, M., *Conservative Essays* (1978).

Crafts, Nicholas, *The Conservative Government's Economic Record: An End of Term Report* (IEA, 1998).

Daykin, Christopher, *Funding the Future? Problems in Pension Reform* (Politeia, 1998).

DSS, *The Abstract of Statistics for Social Security Benefits and Contributions* (1995 edn).

DSS, *Households Below Average Income: A Statistical Analysis 1979–1994/95* (London: The Stationery Office, 1997).

DSS, *National Housing Benefit Accuracy Review 1997–98.*

Elliot, Walter, *Toryism and the Twentieth Century* (1927).

Employment Policy Institute, *Employment Audit*, Issue Nine (Autumn 1998).

European Union, *Business Investment Report* (1998).

Francis, M., and I. Zweiniger-Bargieolowska, *The Conservatives and British Society, 1880–1990* (1996).

Freud, Sigmund, *The Psychopathology of Everyday Life* (1985 edn).

Giddens, Anthony, *The Third Way – The Renewal of Social Democracy* (1998).

Giddens, Anthony, *The Third Way and its Critics* (2000).

Gilmour, Ian, *Inside Right* (1977).

Gosling, A., P. Johnson, J. McCrae and G. Paull, *The Dynamics of Low Pay and Unemployment in Early-1990s Britain* (Institute for Fiscal Studies, 1997).

Gould, Philip, *The Unfinished Revolution* (1998 edn).

Gowland, David, *Banking of Change: Independence, Regulation and the Bank of England* (Politeia, 1997).

Green, David G., *An End to Welfare Rights* (IEA, March 1999).

Green, David G., *Benefit Dependency*, (IEA, January 1999).

Green, E. H. H., *The Crisis of Conservatism: The Politics, Economics and Ideology of the British Conservative Party, 1880–1914* (1995).

Greenleaf, W. H., *The British Political Tradition: The Ideological Heritage* (1983).

Gwartney, James, and Robert Lawson, *Economic Freedom of the World 1998–99 Interim Report* (Vancouver: Fraser Institute, 1998).

Harrison, Wilfrid, *Sources in British Political Thought 1593–1900* (1965 edn).

HM Treasury, *Tax Ready Reckoner and Reliefs* (December 1997).

HM Treasury, *Financial Statement and Budget Report* (March 1998).

HM Treasury, *The Modernisation of Britain's Tax and Benefit System – Number Two; Work Incentives: A Report by Martin Taylor* (March 1998).

HM Treasury Green Paper, *Beating Fraud is Everyone's Business – Securing the Future* (July 1998).

HM Treasury, *Modern Public Services for Britain: Investing in Reform (Comprehensive Spending Review: New Public Spending Plans*

1999–2002), Cm 4011 (July 1998).

HM Treasury, *Pre-Budget Report*, Cm 4076 (November 1998).

HM Treasury, *Pre-Budget Report*, Cm 4917 (November 1998).

HM Treasury, *Economic and Fiscal Strategy Report and Financial Statement and Budget Report*, HC 298 (March 1999).

HM Treasury, *The Modernisation of Britain's Tax and Benefit System – Number Seven; Helping People to Save* (November 2000).

Inland Revenue Statistics (London: The Stationery Office, 1998).

Inland Revenue, *Bicentenary of Income Tax 1799–1999: A Brief History of Income Tax* (December 1998).

International Monetary Fund, *International Financial Statistics Yearbook* (Washington DC: IMF, 1998).

Kariel, Henry S., *Sources in Twentieth-Century Political Thought* (1964).

Kay, John, and Mervyn King, *The British Tax System* (Oxford: Oxford University Press, 5th edn, 1990).

Lawlor, Sheila, *Beveridge or Brown? Contribution and Redistribution: The Real Social Society Debate* (Politeia, 1998).

Lewis, Russell, *The Deadweight State*, Economic Research Council Research Study No. 15 (1998).

Ludlam, Steve, and Martin J. Smith, *Contemporary British Conservatism* (1996).

McCrae, Julian, 'Simplifying the Formal Structure of UK Income Tax', *Fiscal Studies,* vol. 18, no. 3 (Aberdeen: BPC–AUP, 1997).

Market Opinion Research International, *British Public Opinion* (various issues).

Matthews, Kent, *VAT Harmonisation in the EU: Is there a European Laffer Curve for VAT?* (Cardiff: Cardiff Business School, University of Wales, June 1998).

Matthews, Kent, and Jean Lloyd-Williams, *VAT Evasion in Selected Sectors of the Economy: A Preliminary Examination* (Cardiff: Cardiff Business School, University of Wales, 1998).

National Audit Office (NAO), *Audit of Assumptions for the Pre-Budget 2000 Report* (November 2000).

Norton, Philip, *The Conservative Party* (1996).

OECD Economic Outlook, 'Fiscal Consolidation and the Effectiveness of the Public Sector' (Paris: OECD, June 1997).

OECD Economic Outlook (Paris: OECD, June 1998).

OECD Revenue Statistics 1965–1996 (Paris: OECD, 1997).

Office for National Statistics, *Public Finance Trends 96* (London: HMSO, 1996).

Office for National Statistics, *Financial Statistics* (October 1998).

O'Gorman, F., *British Conservatism: Conservative Thought from Burke to Thatcher* (1986).

Osborn, R., *Freud and Marx* (1937).

O'Sullivan, N., *Conservatism* (1976).

Parker, Hermione, *Taxes, Benefits and Family Life*, IEA Research Monograph 50 (1995).

Popper, Karl, *The Open Society and Its Enemies* (1966 edn).

Popper, Karl, *The Poverty of Historicism* (1961 edn).

Ramsden, John, *An Appetite For Power* (1998).

Runciman, W. G., *Social Science and Political Theory* (1965 edn).

Russell, Bertrand, *The Conquest of Happiness* (1987 edn).

Scruton, R., *The Meaning of Conservatism* (1980).

Seldon, A., and S. Bale, *Conservative Century: The Conservative Party Since 1900* (1994).

Smith, J., *The Taming of Democracy: The Conservative Party 1880–1924* (1997).

Stoppard, Tom, *Jumpers* (1972 edn).

Tanzi, Vito, and Ludger Schuknecht, *Public Spending in the 20th Century* (2000).

Tew, Brian, *Wealth and Income* (1965 edn).

Trevelyan, G. M., *British History in the Nineteenth Century and After, 1782–1919* (1937 edn).

Welles, Orson, and Peter Bogdanovich, *This is Orson Welles* (1998 edn).

Willetts, David, *Modern Conservatism* (1992).

Willetts, David, *Why Vote Conservative?* (1997).

Wood, Geoffrey, *Economic Fallacies Exposed* (IEA, October 1997).